THE IMPACT OF SEXUALLY TRANSMITTED DISEASES UPON MARRIAGE

Shaykh Dr. Abdullah al-Tayyār

Member of the General Presidency of Islamic Research and Verdicts in Qasim

ISBN: 978-1-7923-7012-0

First Edition: Shawwal 1442 A.H. / June 2021 C.E.

Cover Design: Aljadeed Design Co.
Website: www.Aljadeed.Design

Translator: Rasheed Barbee

Editing & Formatting: Razan Gregory

Publisher's Information:
Authentic Statements Publishing
P.O. Box 15536
Philadelphia, PA 19131
215.382.3382
215.382.3782 – Fax

Store:
5000 Locust St. (Side Entrance)
Philadelphia, PA 19139
Website: www.authenticstatements.com
E-mail: info@authenticstatements.com

Please visit our website for upcoming publications, audio/DVD online catalog, and info on events and seminars, *inshāAllāh*.

Transliteration Table

Consonants

ء	'	د	d	ض	ḍ	ك	k
ب	b	ذ	dh	ط	ṭ	ل	l
ت	t	ر	r	ظ	ẓ	م	m
ث	th	ز	z	ع	ʿ	ن	n
ج	j	س	s	غ	gh	ه	h
ح	ḥ	ش	sh	ف	f	و	w
خ	kh	ص	ṣ	ق	q	ي	y

Vowels

Short	◌َ	a	◌ِ	i	◌ُ	u
Long	ـَا	ā	ـِي	ī	ـُو	ū
Diphthongs	ـَي	ay	ـَو	aw		

Glyphs

ﷺ *Sallallāhu ʿalayhi wa sallam* (May Allāh's praise & salutations be upon him)

ؑ *ʿAlayhis-salām* (peace be upon him)

ﷻ *ʿAza wa jal* (Mighty and Majestic)

ؓ *RadiyAllāhu ʿanhu* (May Allāh be pleased with him)

ؓ *RadiyAllāhu ʿanha* (May Allāh be pleased with her)

ؓ *RadiyAllāhu ʿanhum* (May Allāh be pleased with them)

ؒ *Rahimahullah* (May Allāh have mercy upon him)

About the Author

He is 'Abdullāh ibn Muḥammad ibn Aḥmad al-Tayyār. He was born during the year 1373 Hijri, which coincides with the year 1954 C.E. Shaykh 'Abdullāh was raised as an orphan in Az-Zulfi, a city in the Riyadh Province of central Saudi Arabia.

After completing his primary education, he attained a bachelor's degree from the *sharī'ah* college in Riyadh in 1395 Hijri. He attained his master's degree from the Higher Judicial Institute in Imām Muḥammad Ibn Saud Islāmic University in 1399 Hijri. Then he attained his doctor's degree from the Higher Judicial Institute in 1402 Hijri.

His scholars include Shaykh 'Abdul 'Azīz ibn Baz, Shaykh 'Uthaymīn, Shaykh Ṣāliḥ Fawzān, and Shaykh Ṣāliḥ al-Aṭram.

He was appointed dean of three colleges at Al-Imām University, then as deputy of the Ministry of Islāmic Affairs and Endowments. Later, he was appointed as a professor at Qassim University and then at Majmaʿah University. Afterward, he became a member of the General Presidency of Islāmic Research and Verdicts in Qassim.

Introduction

Indeed, all the praises belong to Allāh. We praise Him, we seek His assistance, and we seek His forgiveness. We seek refuge in Allāh from the evil of our souls and from the evil of our actions. Whoever Allāh guides, none can misguide him, and whoever is misguided, there is no guide for him. I bear witness that nothing has the right to be worshipped except Allāh, alone, without partners, and I bear witness that Muḥammad is His slave and His Messenger.

﴿ يَا أَيُّهَا الَّذِينَ آمَنُوا اتَّقُوا اللَّهَ حَقَّ تُقَاتِهِ وَلَا تَمُوتُنَّ إِلَّا وَأَنتُم مُّسْلِمُونَ ﴿١٠٢﴾ ﴾

O you who believe! Fear Allāh as He should be feared and die not except in a state of Islām.[1]

---

[1] Sūrah 'Āli 'Imrān 3:102.

﴿ يَا أَيُّهَا النَّاسُ اتَّقُوا رَبَّكُمُ الَّذِي خَلَقَكُم مِّن نَّفْسٍ وَاحِدَةٍ وَخَلَقَ
مِنْهَا زَوْجَهَا وَبَثَّ مِنْهُمَا رِجَالًا كَثِيرًا وَنِسَاءً ۚ وَاتَّقُوا اللَّهَ الَّذِي
تَسَاءَلُونَ بِهِ وَالْأَرْحَامَ ۚ إِنَّ اللَّهَ كَانَ عَلَيْكُمْ رَقِيبًا ﴿١﴾ ﴾

O mankind! Be dutiful to your Lord, Who created you from a single person (Adam), and from him (Adam) He created his wife (Eve), and from them both He created many men and women; and fear Allāh through Whom you demand your mutual rights, and do not cut the relations of kinship. Surely, Allāh is Ever an All-Watcher over you.[1]

﴿ يَا أَيُّهَا الَّذِينَ آمَنُوا اتَّقُوا اللَّهَ وَقُولُوا قَوْلًا سَدِيدًا ﴿٧٠﴾
يُصْلِحْ لَكُمْ أَعْمَالَكُمْ وَيَغْفِرْ لَكُمْ ذُنُوبَكُمْ ۗ وَمَن يُطِعِ اللَّهَ
وَرَسُولَهُ فَقَدْ فَازَ فَوْزًا عَظِيمًا ﴿٧١﴾ ﴾

O you who believe! Fear Allāh and say a word that is correct. He will direct you to do righteous good deeds and will forgive you your sins. And whosoever obeys Allāh and His Messenger, he has indeed achieved a great achievement.[2]

---

[1] Sūrah an-Nisā' 4:1.

[2] Sūrah al-Aḥzāb 33:71.

As to what follows, indeed the esteemed *sharī'ah* of Islām focuses on the interests that benefit the individual, the community, and the Islāmic nation with prosperity and happiness in this life, even before the Hereafter. Allāh (ﷻ) said:

﴿ فَمَنِ اتَّبَعَ هُدَايَ فَلَا يَضِلُّ وَلَا يَشْقَىٰ ١٢٣ ﴾

Then whoever follows My Guidance shall neither go astray nor fall into distress and misery.[1]

It warns against everything that will corrupt the worldly and religious life, and bring about harm and calamities upon the individual, the community, and the Islāmic nation. It especially warns against following the people of falsehood and desires, those that lead the Islāmic nation into perpetual destruction and continuous punishment. Allāh, the Great, spoke the truth. He (ﷻ) said:

﴿ وَلَا تَرْكَنُوا إِلَى الَّذِينَ ظَلَمُوا فَتَمَسَّكُمُ النَّارُ وَمَا لَكُم مِّن دُونِ
اللَّهِ مِنْ أَوْلِيَاءَ ثُمَّ لَا تُنصَرُونَ ١١٣ ﴾

And incline not toward those who do wrong, lest the Fire should touch you, and you have no protectors other than Allāh, nor you would then be helped.[2]

---

[1] Sūrah Ṭāhā 20:123.

[2] Sūrah Hūd 11:113.

Despite warnings from scholars of the *sharī'ah* and medical doctors who caution against falling into that which Allāh (ﷻ) has prohibited, there are many people who are driven by passion and lust to following their desires. Thus, they are faced with the evil consequences, and ruin in this life and the Hereafter.

What we see today of people adorning evil character and bad interactions among each other is only due to their extreme distance from the commands of Allāh (ﷻ) and His prohibitions; as well as their abandonment of the esteemed Sharī'ah that commands toward all good and prohibits all evil.

If we look at our Islāmic *sharī'ah* with a broad view, we find that the goal is to actualize benefit for people. Al-Shaṭibī[1] said, "We learned from examining the *sharī'ah* that it establishes benefit for the people."[2] He then mentioned many verses that prove this statement, like the statement of Allāh (ﷻ):

﴿ وَمَا أَرْسَلْنَاكَ إِلَّا رَحْمَةً لِّلْعَالَمِينَ ١٠٧ ﴾

And We have not sent you, [O Muḥammad], except as a mercy to all the creation.[3]

---

[1] Translator's note: He is the noble scholar 'Abū Isḥāq al-Shaṭibī (720 - 790 A.H.) from Andalusi. Andalusi is now known as the Iberian Peninsula, a mountainous region that is associated with the countries of Spain and Portugal.

[2] Al-Shaṭibī, *Al-Muwafiqaat*, 2/3.

[3] Sūrah al-'Anbiyā' 21:107.

And His statement:

﴿ الَّذِي خَلَقَ الْمَوْتَ وَالْحَيَاةَ لِيَبْلُوَكُمْ أَيُّكُمْ أَحْسَنُ عَمَلًا ﴿٢﴾ ﴾

[He] Who created death and life to test you as to which of you is best in deeds.[1]

He also stated that in many cases, after a particular ruling is mentioned, the reason for this ruling is mentioned afterwards and it clearly states that it is to bring about benefit for the people. An example is in the verse concerning purification for prayer. Allāh (ﷻ) said:

﴿ مَا يُرِيدُ اللَّهُ لِيَجْعَلَ عَلَيْكُم مِّنْ حَرَجٍ وَلَٰكِن يُرِيدُ لِيُطَهِّرَكُمْ وَلِيُتِمَّ نِعْمَتَهُ عَلَيْكُمْ ﴿٦﴾ ﴾

Allāh does not want to place you in difficulty, but He wants to purify you, and to complete His favor on you.[2]

And His statement about fasting. He said:

﴿ يَا أَيُّهَا الَّذِينَ آمَنُوا كُتِبَ عَلَيْكُمُ الصِّيَامُ كَمَا كُتِبَ عَلَى الَّذِينَ مِن قَبْلِكُمْ لَعَلَّكُمْ تَتَّقُونَ ﴿١٨٣﴾ ﴾

---

[1] Sūrah al-Mulk 67:2.

[2] Sūrah al-Mā'idah 5:6.

O you who believe, observing the fasting is prescribed for you as it was prescribed for those before you, that you may become pious.[1]

And He said concerning the prayer:

﴿ إِنَّ الصَّلَاةَ تَنْهَىٰ عَنِ الْفَحْشَاءِ وَالْمُنكَرِ ﴿٤٥﴾ ﴾

Indeed, prayer prohibits immorality and wrongdoing.[2]

He said about the law of equality in punishment:

﴿ وَلَكُمْ فِي الْقِصَاصِ حَيَاةٌ يَا أُولِي الْأَلْبَابِ لَعَلَّكُمْ تَتَّقُونَ ﴿١٧٩﴾ ﴾

And there is for you in legal retribution [saving of] life, O you [people] of understanding, that you may become righteous.[3]

After mentioning these verses as evidence Imām Shaṭibī said, “Since our research has proven this—and this is a beneficial

[1] Sūrah al-Baqarah 2:183.
[2] Sūrah al-‘Ankabūt 29:45.
[3] Sūrah al-Baqarah 2:179.

principle in knowledge—then we are certain that all the commands of the sharīʿah are also to benefit the people."[1]

The *sharīʿah*, in its entirety, is for benefit. It either repels a harm or brings about a benefit. When you hear the statement of Allāh (ﷻ), "O you who believe," then ponder the advice of Allāh (ﷻ) after His call to the believers. You will only find good that He is inciting them toward, evil that He is preventing them from, or both a command and a prohibition. Allāh (ﷻ) has explained the harms found in some of the prohibitions in order to incite the people to avoid them. Likewise, He has mentioned the benefits found within His commands to incite the people to implement them.

For this reason, I decided to write about some important topics related to the Muslim woman, which I have outlined in my research. I ask Allāh (ﷻ) to benefit me and my brothers by way of this and to make it an argument on our behalf, not against us. And our final supplication is "All praises belong to Allāh, the Lord of al that exists."

Dr. ʿAbdullāh ibn Muḥammad ibn Aḥmad al-Tayyar
Professor at the University of Qassim
1428 Hijri

---

[1] Al-Shaṭibī, *Al-Muwafiqaat*, 2/4.

Research Summary

Looking at the reality of the world today, from the advancement of material civilization and the ease by which the various nations of the world become acquainted with one another, we see that people in every corner of the world are able to connected as individuals and communities. This vast technical advancement delivers everything good and bad to all nations of the world such that the traditions, manners, and customs of the Muslims have been greatly affected. Some Muslims imitate the West in everything big and small. Some Muslim youth travel to Western countries—where pornography and homosexuality are widespread—and intermingle with individuals in these countries through work, study, or vacation. Due to the weak religious faith of most of these youth, they fall into the sin of mixing with the women of these countries who are carrying many sexually transmitted diseases that have appeared during recent times. These diseases have spread like wildfire due to the masses of people indulging in fornication.

When the Islāmic scholars noticed the danger of this affair and the prevalence of these diseases among the children of the Islāmic nation, they rushed to clarify the danger of this affair to the Muslims in an effort to warn them against falling into its clutches. Thus, the Muslims can safeguard their bodies and their health from these dangerous diseases.

In the interest of clarifying some issues connected to the Muslim woman regarding marriage to a husband infected with a disease and pregnancy while infected with a disease, I conducted my research. Allāh (ﷻ) spoke the truth when He said:

﴿ فَلْيَحْذَرِ الَّذِينَ يُخَالِفُونَ عَنْ أَمْرِهِ أَن تُصِيبَهُمْ فِتْنَةٌ أَوْ يُصِيبَهُمْ عَذَابٌ أَلِيمٌ ﴿٦٣﴾ ﴾

And let those who oppose the Messenger beware, lest some trials befall them, or a painful torment be inflicted on them.[1]

The Prophet (ﷺ) said:

يَا مَعْشَرَ الْمُهَاجِرِينَ خَمْسٌ إِذَا ابْتُلِيتُمْ بِهِنَّ وَأَعُوذُ بِاللَّهِ أَنْ تُدْرِكُوهُنَّ لَمْ تَظْهَرِ الْفَاحِشَةُ فِي قَوْمٍ قَطُّ حَتَّى يُعْلِنُوا بِهَا إِلاَّ فَشَا فِيهِمُ الطَّاعُونُ وَالأَوْجَاعُ الَّتِي لَمْ تَكُنْ مَضَتْ فِي أَسْلاَفِهِمُ الَّذِينَ مَضَوْا . وَلَمْ يَنْقُصُوا الْمِكْيَالَ وَالْمِيزَانَ إِلاَّ أُخِذُوا

[1] Sūrah an-Nūr 24:63.

بِالسِّنِينَ وَشِدَّةِ الْمَؤُنَةِ وَجَوْرِ السُّلْطَانِ عَلَيْهِمْ . وَلَمْ يَمْنَعُوا زَكَاةَ أَمْوَالِهِمْ إِلاَّ مُنِعُوا
الْقَطْرَ مِنَ السَّمَاءِ وَلَوْلاَ الْبَهَائِمُ لَمْ يُمْطَرُوا وَلَمْ يَنْقُضُوا عَهْدَ اللَّهِ وَعَهْدَ رَسُولِهِ إِلاَّ
سَلَّطَ اللَّهُ عَلَيْهِمْ عَدُوًّا مِنْ غَيْرِهِمْ فَأَخَذُوا بَعْضَ مَا فِي أَيْدِيهِمْ . وَمَا لَمْ تَحْكُمْ
أَئِمَّتُهُمْ بِكِتَابِ اللَّهِ وَيَتَخَيَّرُوا مِمَّا أَنْزَلَ اللَّهُ إِلاَّ جَعَلَ اللَّهُ بَأْسَهُمْ بَيْنَهُمْ

O Muhajirun, there are five things with which you will be tested, and I seek refuge with Allāh lest you live to see them. Immorality never appears among a people to such an extent that they commit it openly, except plagues and diseases that were never known among the predecessors will spread among them. They do not cheat in weights and measures, except they will be stricken with famine, severe calamity and the oppression of their rulers. They do not withhold the *zakāt* of their wealth, except rain will be withheld from the sky, and were it not for the animals, no rain would fall on them. They do not break their covenant with Allāh and His Messenger, except Allāh will enable their enemies to overpower them and take some of what is in their hands. Unless their leaders rule according to the Book of Allāh and seek all good from that which Allāh has revealed, Allāh will cause them to fight one another.[1]

We ask Allāh (ﷻ) to preserve our religion and our well-being, and to protect our sons and daughters from every evil and calamity.

---

[1] *Sunān Ibn Mājah* 4019.

Research Outline:

- First Research: Medical Examination before Marriage to the Extent of Mandating Testing before Marriage
  - First Discussion: The Ruler Mandating Testing
  - Second discussion: The Guardian of the Woman Mandating Testing
- Second Research: Marriage to Someone with an Infectious Disease
  - First Discussion: If Only One Person Has an Infectious Disease
  - Second Discussion: If Both People Have an Infectious Disease
- Third Research: Intimacy with a Spouse That Has an Infectious Disease
  - First Discussion: Intimacy without Intercourse
  - Second Discussion: Utilizing Protection during Intimacy
- Fourth Research: Pregnancy of a Woman with an Infectious Disease
- Fifth Research: Is It Permissible to Abort the Pregnancy of a Woman with an Infectious Disease?

- ∴ First Discussion: Abortion before the First Forty Days of Pregnancy
- ∴ Second Discussion: Abortion after the First Forty Days of Pregnancy, before the Soul Is Breathed into the Fetus
- ∴ Third Discussion: Abortion after the Soul Is Breathed into the Fetus

❖ Sixth Research: Sustainability of Marriage with an Infectious Disease

- ∴ First Discussion: Sustainability When Only One of the Spouses Has an Infectious Disease
- ∴ Second Discussion: Sustainability When Both Spouses Have an Infectious Disease

❖ Seventh Research: Separating the Spouses If One or Both of Them Have an Infectious Disease

- ∴ First Discussion: The Wife Who Does Not Have an Infectious Disease Request a Separation
- ∴ Second Discussion: The Husband Who Does Not Have an Infectious Disease Requesting Compensation upon Divorcing His Wife

❖ Eighth Research: A Parent with an Infectious Disease Raising a Child That Does Not Have an Infectious Disease

- First Discussion: A Healthy Mother Raising a Child That Has an Infectious Disease

- Second Discussion: A Father with a Disease Raising a Healthy Child

First Research: Medical Examination

Before delving into this topic, I wanted to explain the importance of the blessing of marriage and how it is a sign from the signs of Allāh (ﷻ) that prove His greatness and power. Indeed, the wisdom of Allāh (ﷻ) necessitates that He give each male and female specific characteristics that strengthen the bond between them in order to achieve physical and psychological tranquility after marriage. The physical strength of each of them has a positive or negative effect upon the sexual interaction that Allāh (ﷻ) prescribed for them through permissible copulation. Allāh (ﷻ) explained this in His statement:

﴿ هُوَ الَّذِي خَلَقَكُم مِّن نَّفْسٍ وَاحِدَةٍ وَجَعَلَ مِنْهَا زَوْجَهَا لِيَسْكُنَ إِلَيْهَا ١٨٩ ﴾

It is He Who has created you from a single person (Adam), and (then) He has created from him his

> **wife (Eve), in order that he might enjoy the pleasure of living with her.[1]**

And His statement:

﴿ وَمِنْ آيَاتِهِ أَنْ خَلَقَ لَكُم مِّنْ أَنفُسِكُمْ أَزْوَاجًا لِّتَسْكُنُوا إِلَيْهَا وَجَعَلَ بَيْنَكُم مَّوَدَّةً وَرَحْمَةً ۚ إِنَّ فِي ذَٰلِكَ لَآيَاتٍ لِّقَوْمٍ يَتَفَكَّرُونَ ﴿٢١﴾ ﴾

> **And among His Signs is this, that He created for you wives from among yourselves, that you may find repose in them, and He has placed between you affection and mercy. Verily, in that are indeed signs for a people who reflect.[2]**

The Messenger of Allāh (ﷺ) confirmed the importance of this bond and how it has been established to protect the Muslims from falling into the traps that Allāh (ﷻ) has prohibited them from. And we see the instruction the Prophet (ﷺ) gave to the woman who denies her husband his rights and the effects of that. He (ﷺ) said:

وَالَّذِى نَفْسِى بِيَدِهِ مَا مِنْ رَجُلٍ يَدْعُو امْرَأَتَهُ إِلَى فِرَاشِهَا فَتَأْبَى عَلَيْهِ إِلاَّ كَانَ الَّذِى فِى السَّمَاءِ سَاخِطًا عَلَيْهَا حَتَّى يَرْضَى عَنْهَا

---

[1] Sūrah al-'A'rāf 7:189.

[2] Sūrah ar-Rūm 30:21.

I swear by the One who has my soul in His Hand, there is no man who calls his wife to the bed and she refuses except that the One who is above the heavens is angry with her until her husband is pleased with her.[1]

Just as the husband has the right to enjoy living with his wife, the wife also has the same right, as has been clarified in the Book of Allāh (ﷻ) and the *sunnah* of the Messenger of Allāh (ﷺ).

Marriage also has another intended purpose, and that is to produce offspring. Allāh (ﷻ) said:

﴿ وَاللَّهُ جَعَلَ لَكُم مِّنْ أَنفُسِكُمْ أَزْوَاجًا وَجَعَلَ لَكُم مِّنْ أَزْوَاجِكُم بَنِينَ وَحَفَدَةً ﴿٧٢﴾ ﴾

And Allāh has made for you wives of your own kind, and has made for you, from your wives, sons and grandchildren.[2]

The Messenger of Allāh (ﷺ) said:

تَزَوَّجُوا الْوَدُودَ الْوَلُودَ إِنِّي مُكَاثِرٌ بِكُمُ الْأَنْبِيَاءَ يَوْمَ الْقِيَامَةِ

[1] "Book of Marriage," *Muslim*, 120.

[2] Sūrah an-Naḥl 16:72.

Marry the women who are loving and fertile, for indeed by way of you I shall have a greater number than the Prophets on the Day of Judgment.[1]

There is no doubt that when the Messenger of Allāh (ﷺ) commanded marriage and childbearing, he was aware of the impact having an abundance of offspring has upon making a nation strong and protected. The advantages of a large nation outweight those of a small nation.

Another goal of marriage is for people to live upon the earth. Populating the earth is what Allāh (ﷻ) intended for His creation. In fact, it is at the forefront of what was intended for them. This is because the purpose for creation is for the creation to worship Allāh (ﷻ) alone without partners, and this purpose cannot be actualized except by way of them living upon the earth. And they cannot live upon the earth unless they produce offspring. Allāh (ﷻ) said:

﴿ هُوَ أَنشَأَكُم مِّنَ الْأَرْضِ وَاسْتَعْمَرَكُمْ فِيهَا ﴿٦١﴾ ﴾

He brought you forth from the earth and settled you therein.[2]

---

[1] *Sunān an-Nasā'ī* 3227.

[2] Sūrah Hūd 11:61.

Living upon the earth necessitates the presence of mankind, with strong bodies and strong intellects. Therefore, marriage—with its honorable purposes—achieves the permanence of offspring and saves nations from deterioration and weakness that causes their death and extinction.

However, in recent times, problems have arisen between the spouses—some of them mental and some physical. Scholars, past and present, have discussed some of these problems such as male and female castration, vaginal atresia,[1] dementia, impotence, spinal cord disease, and leprosy. The scholars have discussed these illnesses, as well as other diseases, and given verdicts for each one. Some illnesses require a marriage annulment, while others have different, specific rulings.

With the passage of time, development of human concepts, and large number of social problems that result in calamities, it is necessary to deal with these issues based upon the correct understanding and belief system. Among these calamities is the concept of genetics and the discovery of many infectious diseases.

[1] Translator's note: Vaginal atresia is a condition in which the vagina is abnormally closed or absent.

The sequence of the human genome has identified genetic factors within the human being, and these genes numbered in the thousands.[1]

The discovery of these diseases, at the present time and with the advancement of medicine and research, opens the way to knowing the correct ways to treat them, especially infectious diseases. Islām deals with the treatment of diseases that occur between the husband and wife by preventing them before they occur, and by immunization of individuals to prevent the spread of disease whether it is hereditary or contagious.

The responsibility in this regard falls on the person himself, so that he does not expose himself to the causes that lead to the disease. The responsibility also lies with the leaders of that country. They must prevent their citizens from being exposed to infectious diseases by imposing safety measures for everyone.

The basic principles for this protection are the legal directives from the Book of Allāh (ﷻ) and the Sunnah of His Messenger (ﷺ). These directives are tremendous if the people adhere to them and implement them in the proper manner.

---

[1] Translator's note: An international research effort called the Human Genome Project, which worked to determine the sequence of the human genome and identify the genes that it contains, estimated that humans have between 20,000 and 25,000 genes. Every person has two copies of each gene, one inherited from each parent. (Source: National Human Genome Research Institute).

As for the directives from the Book of Allāh, Allāh (ﷻ) commanded us to supplicate to Him for righteous offspring.

﴿ رَبِّ هَبْ لِي مِن لَّدُنكَ ذُرِّيَّةً طَيِّبَةً ۖ إِنَّكَ سَمِيعُ الدُّعَاءِ ﴿٣٨﴾ ﴾

O my Lord! Grant me from You a good offspring. You are indeed the All-Hearer of invocation.[1]

And He (ﷻ) said:

﴿ وَالَّذِينَ يَقُولُونَ رَبَّنَا هَبْ لَنَا مِنْ أَزْوَاجِنَا وَذُرِّيَّاتِنَا قُرَّةَ أَعْيُنٍ ﴿٧٤﴾ ﴾

And those who say, "Our Lord! Bestow on us from our wives and our offspring who will be the comfort of our eyes."[2]

As for the Sunnah, the Prophet (ﷺ) said:

تَخَيَّرُوا لِنُطَفِكُمْ وَانْكِحُوا الأَكْفَاءَ وَأَنْكِحُوا إِلَيْهِمْ

---

[1] Sūrah 'Āli 'Imrān 3:38.
[2] Sūrah al-Furqān 25:74.

Choose the best for your semen and marry compatible women and give them away in marriage.[1]

This proves you should select a good wife and a good husband in terms of their religious commitment and their physical characteristics, as this will have a major effect upon the offspring.

A man[2] came to the Prophet (ﷺ), after his wife gave birth to a black son, because neither he nor his wife was black. He intended to deny this child. The man said:

فَقَالَ يَا رَسُولَ اللَّهِ وُلِدَ لِي غُلاَمٌ أَسْوَدُ. فَقَالَ هَلْ لَكَ مِنْ إِبِلٍ؟" قال: نعم. قال: "فَمَا أَلْوَانُهَا؟" قال: فيها الأحمر والأسود وغير ذلك. قال: "فَأَنَّى ذَلِكَ؟" قال: عرقٌ نَزع. وقال: "وَهَذَا عِرْقٌ نَزَع

A man went to the Prophet and said, "O Messenger of Allāh, a black child has been born to me." The Prophet said, "Do you have camels?" The man said, "Yes." The Prophet said, "What color are they?" The man said, "They are red and black." The Prophet said, "How is that?" The man said, "Hereditary." The Prophet said, "And this is hereditary."[3]

Some old women from the Tribe of Bani 'Ajal informed him that his wife's grandmother was black.

---

[1] *Ibn Mājah* 2928, declared authentic by al-Albanī in *As-Ṣaḥīḥ* 3/56.

[2] Translator's note: He is the noble companion Ḍaumḍaum ibn Qatādah (ﷺ).

[3] *Ṣaḥīḥ al-Bukhārī* 5305.

Newborns are being born with many disabilities. Thus, it becomes clear that perhaps the husband or wife may have committed some sins such as fornication, drinking alcohol, smoking, or other things that could have caused the deformity in their offspring.

When the jurists spoke about diseases and their effect on the relationship between spouses, many of these diseases were not discovered. Along with great scientific advancements, came the discovery of many other diseases, some of which are dangerous and others that are not. These diseases can be transferred from one person to another by means of infection. If these diseases are not curtailed to prevent spreading, this can lead to a catastrophic epidemic that will affect future generations and cause destruction of the health, economic, and social lives of nations.

In order to avoid these diseases, it is mandatory upon us to take measures to prevent them through medical examination of those who want to marry, before their marriage so that each of them is aware of the situation of the other.

Through this examination, it is possible to know which diseases can be overlooked, or whether it is best that they find someone who is compatible with them physically and psychologically.

The people from earlier generations were honest when it came to mentioning their psychological and physical faults. They lived simple lives; thus, there was no need to verify or conduct a thorough examination before marriage.

An example of the people of old explaining their situation before marriage is the *ḥadīth* of Umm Salamah.

It was narrated from Umm Salamah that when her *'iddah* period had ended, 'Abū Bakr sent word to her proposing marriage, but she did not marry him. Then the Messenger of Allāh (ﷺ) sent 'Umar bin Al-Khaṭṭāb with a proposal of marriage. She said:

أَخْبِرْ رَسُولَ اللَّهِ صلى الله عليه وسلم أَنِّي امْرَأَةٌ غَيْرَى وَأَنِّي امْرَأَةٌ مُصْبِيَةٌ وَلَيْسَ أَحَدٌ مِنْ أَوْلِيَائِي شَاهِدٌ

"Tell the Messenger of Allāh that I am a jealous woman and that I have sons, and none of my guardians are present."

He went to the Messenger of Allāh (ﷺ) and told him that. He said, "Go back to her and tell her:

أَمَّا قَوْلُكِ إِنِّي امْرَأَةٌ غَيْرَى فَسَأَدْعُو اللَّهَ لَكِ فَيُذْهِبُ غَيْرَتَكِ وَأَمَّا قَوْلُكِ إِنِّي امْرَأَةٌ مُصْبِيَةٌ فَسَتُكْفَيْنَ صِبْيَانَكِ وَأَمَّا قَوْلُكِ أَنْ لَيْسَ أَحَدٌ مِنْ أَوْلِيَائِي شَاهِدٌ فَلَيْسَ أَحَدٌ مِنْ أَوْلِيَائِكِ شَاهِدٌ وَلاَ غَائِبٌ يَكْرَهُ ذَلِكَ

> **As for your saying that you are a jealous woman, I will pray to Allāh for you to take away your jealousy. As for your saying that you have sons, your sons will be taken care of. And as for your saying that none of your guardians are present, none of your guardians, present or absent, would object to that."**

She said to her son 'Umar:

يَا عُمَرُ ، قُمْ فَزَوِّجْ رَسُولَ اللَّهِ

"O 'Umar, stand and marry me to the Messenger of Allāh."

Thus, her son 'Umar[1] performed the marriage.[2]

During our present time, there is a decline in trustworthiness and honesty due to the people being far away from the noble Islāmic morals that every Muslim must adorn themselves with. Thus, with the advancement of science, there are medical precautions in place to ensure the safety of the spouses from diseases. Also, many countries have enacted laws to make premarital medical examinations mandatory.

What is the Islāmic *sharī'ah* position on this issue? To make this matter clear, we first present the medical position.

---

[1] Translator's note: Her son, 'Umar, is mentioned in the following famous narration. 'Umar bin 'Abū Salamah said, "I was a boy under the care of the Messenger of Allah (ﷺ), and as my hand used to wander around in the dish, he (ﷺ) said to me once, 'Mention the Name of Allah, eat with your right hand, and eat from what is in front of you.'" (*Al-Bukhārī and Muslim*).

[2] *Sunān an-Nasā'ī* 3254.

Medical Examination Before Marriage from a Medical Point of View

The negatives and positives of conducting a medical examination before marriage have been studied. After studying this issue, the opinions are as follows.

The Pros of Medical Examinations before Marriage

1. These examinations are considered remarkably effective as a preventive means to reduce dangerous hereditary and infectious diseases.

2. Examinations protect society by reducing the spread of disease. Consequently, this reduces physical harm, as well as economic harm upon individuals, families, and societies. When a large percentage of the society is disabled, their humanitarian and financial needs are greater than those without disabilities.

3. Examinations help to ensure the birth of children who are mentality and physically healthy.

4. To some extent, premarital examinations can determine the ability of spouses to have children.

5. Examinations can verify the ability of each spouse to have a healthy sexual relationship with the other, in a way that naturally satisfies each others' desires. These examinations

also test for the presence of organic disorders or pathophysiological diseases.

6. Examinations can verify the absence of chronic diseases that can affect life after marriage, such as cancer and other things that play a role in disrupting the stability of marital life.

7. Examinations help to ensure each spouse is not harmed by the other during intimacy, by ensuring each of them is free from sexual transmitted diseases and other epidemics.

The Cons of Medical Examinations before Marriage

1. Medical examinations can cause frustration within the society. If the tests prove that there is a possibility for a woman to be infertile, or if she is diagnosed with breast cancer and others know about it, this will cause her psychological and social damage. This can damage her future, especially because test results can be right or wrong.

2. Examinations can cause anxiety, depression, and a feeling of hopeless if they are told they have an incurable disease.

3. Many of the test results are based upon a theory of probability. And they do not provide a true guide for detecting future diseases.

4. Negative test results deprived some people of the opportunity to marry, and the results may not be accurate.

5. Rarely is a person free from disease, especially when we understand that over 3,000 single-gene, or monogenic, diseases have been identified.

6. Rushing to give medical advice after the examination can cause more harm than good.

7. The people who present themselves for testing may be harmed if the testers maliciously divulge their test results.

In spite of these negatives, the medical opinion inclines toward the necessity of conducting such examinations for those who wish to have them. Accordingly, the doctor is obliged at that time and upon the request of the suitors to give medical advice.

As for when people are obliged and forced to undergo a medical examination, the medical opinion points to the necessity of identifying certain types of diseases. This is to limit the spread of some hereditary diseases, so the bearer of the disease can be detected before marriage and the potential children can be protected. These diseases are few and known to be medically hereditary. Also, the possibility of reaching the carrier from the parents is known scientifically and medically.

Medical Examination Before Marriage from the Sharīʿah Point of View

Contemporary scholars have studied this topic from various angles and explained its importance from the standpoint of the *sharīʿah*.

Their opinions coincided with the doctors to a large extent. Some of the scholars have said that premarital medical testing does not contradict with Islāmic law or the intent of marriage. Marriage between healthy people lasts longer than marriage between sick people. And the examination can be arranged such that it does not harm the man or the woman.

Some doctors have stated that medical examinations are necessary. Ṣābūni said, "It is not hidden from anyone, the harm of one spouse afflicted with an infectious disease transmitting the illness to their mate. It also involves deception, because if the healthy spouse knew this beforehand, perhaps they would not have agreed to the marriage. Thus, my suggestion is that in addition to requiring a testimony of good character before marriage, there should also be a blood test given from each potential spouse. Modern medicine has proven with an accurate analysis that if the mother's blood type is not compatible with the father's blood type, this can result in a miscarriage or deformities within the child, or the child may grow up sickly. A medical examination of the blood of both potential spouses can determine this. A medical examination does not delay marriage, but it gives a clear picture for each person about their future partner. Islāmic law accepts everything that is beneficial for the individual and the family in this regard, even if it is not stipulated by the jurists specifically.""[1]

[1] The ruling of marriage in light of Islamic jurisprudence.

Translator's addendum: If a woman who is Rh-negative and a man who is Rh-positive conceive a baby, the fetus may inherit Rh-positive blood from the father. If a woman is Rh-negative and her baby is Rh-positive, the woman's body can react to the Rh-positive protein as a foreign object substance, sending antibodies across the placenta to attack her baby's red blood cells. This is known as Rh incompatibility. (Dr. Armando Fuentes, MD) *End of translator's addendum.*

Some doctors believe genetic testing is part of premarital examination and these tests should be conducted before marriage. Doctor ʻĀrif ʻAlī ʻĀrif said, "These tests may bring about a legitimate benefit while preventing an anticipated harm. This does not contradict the decree of Allāh; rather, it is from the decree of Allāh. A genetic analysis is useful, especially in families that have a genetic history of disease. If a person is expected to be affected, this expectation is similar to a reality which actually has occurred. The *sharīʻah* takes precaution from those things that occur frequently."

There are scholars who view premarital examinations as permissible, but in some cases unnecessary. In some of his verdicts, the noble scholar Shaykh ʻAbdul ʻAzīz ibn Baz said these tests are not needed. He said, "I encourage those who are pursing marriage to have a good thought about Allāh (ﷻ).

أَنَا عِنْدَ ظَنِّ عَبْدِي بِي

I am to My slave as he thinks of Me.[1]

And these tests may produce results that are incorrect."[2]

What I see is that the opinion of our Eminence Shaykh ibn Baz is correct on this issue. The opinion that medical examination is permissible is also correct. Trusting Allāh (ﷻ) does not contradict taking the necessary means. There is no better proof than the statement of 'Umar ibn Al-Khaṭṭāb (رضي الله عنه). When the plague of Sham occurred, he said, "We are fleeing from the decree of Allāh to the decree of Allāh."[3]

As for the accuracy of test results, modern medicine has proven its ability to detect many infectious and hereditary diseases. Many diseases can be treated before they negatively affect the spouses or offspring. If there remains a possibility that a spouse may be affected, the *sharī'ah* takes the same precaution for something that happens frequently as it does for something that has already occurred.

But when we say that premarital testing is permissible, it must be noted that this does not in any way prevent those who are proposing to marry from continuing on with the marriage after

---

[1] *Ṣaḥīḥ al-Bukhārī* 7505.

[2] *Muslims Newspaper* 597.

[3] *Ṣaḥīḥ al-Bukhārī* 5288.

knowing certain defects are present. This is because the examination process does not nullify the freedom of those who are proposing to marry from accepting the marriage despite the presence of defects.

Evidence for the Permissibility of Medical Examinations

1. The Islāmic *sharī'ah* calls for preservation of the lineage. It is from the five basic human necessities Islām safeguards (religion, life, lineage, intellect, and wealth). The prophets (ﷺ) supplicated to Allāh (ﷻ) that He would grant them good offspring. Allāh (ﷻ) said about Zakariya (ﷺ):

﴿ قَالَ رَبِّ هَبْ لِي مِن لَّدُنكَ ذُرِّيَّةً طَيِّبَةً ۖ إِنَّكَ سَمِيعُ الدُّعَاءِ ﴿٣٨﴾ ﴾

O my Lord grant me from You a good offspring, You are indeed the All-Hearer of invocation.[1]

The offspring will not be good unless they are free from physical defects.

2. Preserving the entity of marriage. 'Umar ibn al-Khaṭṭāb (ﷺ) said, "If a man marries a woman who is insane, has leprosy, or

[1] Sūrah 'Āli 'Imrān 3:38.

albinism—without being told of her condition by her guardian—and he copulates with her, she keeps her bride-money in its entirety and her husband has damages against her guardian.[1] Therefore, the medical examination preserves the marital entity from permissible annulment that would be based upon deception, according to the opinion of some jurists.

Translator's addendum: Imām Mālik further explained this narration by saying, "The husband has damages against her guardian when the guardian is her father, brother, or one who is deemed to have knowledge of her condition. If the guardian who gives her in marriage is a nephew, or a member of her tribe who is not deemed to have knowledge of her condition, there are no damages against him. The woman returns what she has taken of her bride-money and the husband leaves her whatever amount is thought to be fair."[2]

3. There is general evidence saying those with infectious diseases should be avoided. The Prophet (ﷺ) said:

لاَ يُورِدُ الْمُمْرِضُ عَلَى الْمُصِحِّ

Do not allow the sick camels to drink alongside the healthy ones.[3]

---

[1] *Muwaṭṭā' Mālik* 1102.

[2] *Muwaṭṭā' Mālik* 1102.

[3] *Sunan Ibn Mājah* 3670.

And his statement:

لاَ عَدْوَى وَلاَ طِيَرَةَ وَلاَ هَامَةَ وَلاَ صَفَرَ ، وَفِرَّ مِنَ الْمَجْذُومِ كَمَا تَفِرُّ مِنَ الأَسَدِ

There is no *'adwā* (transmission of infectious disease without the permission of Allāh) and no *ṭīyarah* (superstitious belief in bird omens), nor is there any *hāmah* (an owl or the bones of a dead person turned into a bird that could fly), nor is there any bad omen in the month of Ṣafar, and one should run away from the leper as one runs away from a lion.[1]

The infectious diseases can only be known by way of examinations.

4. The Prophet (ﷺ) directed the husband towards selecting a wife whose family is known to bear children. He said:

تَزَوَّجُوا الْوَدُودَ الْوَلُودَ إِنِّي مُكَاثِرٌ بِكُمُ الأَنْبِيَاءَ يَوْمَ الْقِيَامَةِ

Marry the women who are loving and fertile, for indeed by way of you I shall have a greater number than the prophets on the Day of Judgment.[2]

This indicates the importance of selecting a spouse on the basis of the health of the offspring and the future birth.

---

[1] *Ṣaḥīḥ al-Bukhārī* 5707.

[2] *Sunān an-Nasā'ī* 3227.

5. The Prophet (ﷺ) encouraging the man desiring to marry to look at the potential spouse. 'Abū Huraira said that a man came to the Prophet (ﷺ) and told him he had contracted to marry a woman of the 'Anṣār, to which he replied:

فَانْظُرْ إِلَيْهَا فَإِنَّ فِي أَعْيُنِ الأَنْصَارِ شَيْئًا

Then look at her, for there is something in the eyes of the 'Anṣār.[1] (Meaning that some of them have features which cause aversion.)

This indicates the need to know the flaws of the fiancé, and the guardian must mention these issues.

6. The scholars who follow the schools of thought of Mālik, Shāfiʿī, and Ḥanbalī, say that the marriage contract is similar to other civil contracts. Thus there is the choice to annul the transaction or the marriage if a defect is found that was not mentioned. But they differ concerning the extent of the defect that allows the marriage to be annulled. This indicates the obligation of each suitor to reveal their defects so the marriage will not be annulled, because the annulment of the marriage will result in material and psychological harm.

7. Some scholars prefer marriage to strangers as opposed to relatives. They prefer that a man not marry his paternal or maternal cousins to avoid weakening the child. 'Umar ibn al-

[1] *Mishkāt al-Maṣābīḥ* 3098.

Khaṭṭāb said, "You have become slim (weak), thus marry strangers."

8. The medical examination serves the interests of the new spouse, the family, and society. It wards off corruption on the social and economic level.

9. The means to achieve a goal take the same ruling as the goal. Thus, if the goal is to preserve the mental and physical integrity of the individual, then the means of this goal are legitimate.

10. There are some diseases that are frightening and the spouses are afraid of them, so embarking on marriage without knowing the other person's health is harmful. The Prophet (ﷺ) said:

لاَ ضَرَرَ وَلاَ ضِرَارَ

There should be neither harming nor reciprocating harm.[1]

From the aforementioned, it can be said that the medical examination is something that is not opposed by Islāmic law. Rather, it supports it because of the many interests that it contains for individuals, families and societies.

[1] *Sunān Ibn Mājah* 2341.

First Discussion: The Ruler Mandating Testing

Can the necessity of premarital examination reach the point where the ruler mandates it and makes it compulsory? If the leader of a country wants to mandate testing during a time when certain diseases are spreading in specific countries, and marriage is from the reasons this disease is spreading, then it is permissible for him to mandate testing as part of his politics and law. However, this mandate, even if it is legally binding or results in financial penalties, does not affect the validity of the marriage contract. The marriage contract is valid when all the conditions of the marriage are fulfilled.

As for forcing people to undergo a comprehensive, detailed medical examination, in addition to its high financial cost it leads to negative results such that the harms outweigh the benefits. Consequently, the medical examination can turn into a harmful tool. But there is nothing wrong with both suitors undergoing a comprehensive, detailed medical examination if this is what both parties want.

Second Discussion: The Guardian of the Woman Mandating Testing

Guardian (*Walī*) according to the language: The origin of the guardian refers to a relative. It means a helper. The term guardian (*walī*) can refer to kindship, a leader, or a sultan over a country. The guardian of the woman seeking marriage is the one who is responsible for her marriage contract. He does not abandon her to manage the marriage contract without him.

Guardian according to the religious meaning: The guardianship is the establishment of an adult person to manage the personal affairs of others. The jurists differ regarding the obligation of having a guardian for the marriage contract. There are different opinions, and the most correct of them is the view of the majority of scholars from the Mālikī, Shāfi'ī, Ḥanbalī, and Ibn Ḥazm schools of thought. Their view is that one of the conditions for the validity of the marriage contract is the presence of the woman's guardian to approve of the individual who presents himself for marriage. Consequently, the marriage contract is not valid without the presence of the guardian. This is based upon the statement of the Prophet (ﷺ). He said:

لَا نِكَاحَ إِلَّا بِوَلِيٍّ

There is no marriage without a guardian.[1]

For this reason, the All-Wise Legislator has commanded the guardian to investigate the interest of the woman under his care by marrying her to someone who is compatible. This means marrying her to someone who is similar to her and free from those defects that would lead to annulment of the marriage. It is in the best interest of the woman that her guardian requests that the

---

[1] *Mishkāt al-Maṣābīḥ* 3130.

suitor present a medical examination confirming that he is free from contagious diseases. This interest is included in his guardianship. This is from the permissible conditions which the guardian can stipulate.

The jurists have argued that compatibility is the right of the woman and the guardian. She has the right to protect herself from the humiliation of a man who marries her to belittle her and from those who do not equal her in qualities of competence. Thus, she has the right to refuse someone who is not compatible with her. The scholars have stated that from the qualities of compatibility is to be free from defects.

Ibn Rushd from the Mālikīs said, "Being compatible means they are equal in terms of health, and free from those major defects."[1] Scholars of the Shāfiʿī school of thought have said that compatibility is to be free of those faults that would allow the annulment of the marriage. Therefore, if a man suffers from defects such as insanity, leprosy, and albinism, he is not compatible for a woman who is free from these defects. This is because the soul dislikes the companionship of the person with this, and the intent of marriage will be broken even if she also has a type of defect. If they have different defects, they are still not compatible. If they have different defects but his defect is worse, the same applies. If her defect is worse, or if they are equal, the same applies. This is

---

[1] *Sharḥ al-Kabīr* 2/249.

because a person will dislike another person in a way he will not dislike himself. This applies to the man who was born without a reproductive organ—or has been castrated—and the woman whose reproductive passage is closed."

Being free of defects only applies to the two spouses specifically and it does not apply to their parents. Thus, the child whose father has leprosy is equal to the child whose father does not have leprosy.

'Umar ibn al-Khaṭṭāb (ﷺ) sent a man to the watering station for those performing *Ḥajj*. While there, the man married a woman and the man was sterile. 'Umar said to him, "Did you inform her that you are sterile?" The man replied, "No." 'Umar said, "Inform her and give her the choice to stay or leave."[1]

Based on that, it is the right of the woman's guardian to request that the man proposing marriage present test results to reassure them that he is free from infectious and genetic diseases that could harm the woman. The Prophet (ﷺ) said:

أَلاَ كُلُّكُمْ رَاعٍ، وَكُلُّكُمْ مَسْئُولٌ عَنْ رَعِيَّتِهِ

All of you are shepherds and all of you will be questioned about their flock.[2]

---

[1] Zād al-Ma'ād 5/165.

[2] Ṣaḥīḥ al-Bukhārī 7138.

These premarital examinations are from the permissible conditions permitted by the Sharīʻah. If the guardian of the woman requests that the man proposing marriage take an examination, then it is upon him to fulfill the request and abide by it if he wants to get married. This is based upon the statement of the Prophet (ﷺ):

الْمُسْلِمُونَ عَلَى شُرُوطِهِمْ

The Muslims must uphold their conditions.[1]

And his statement:

أَحَقُّ مَا أَوْفَيْتُمْ مِنَ الشُّرُوطِ أَنْ تُوفُوا بِهِ مَا اسْتَحْلَلْتُمْ بِهِ الْفُرُوجَ

The stipulations most entitled to be abided by are those which make sexual relations permissible.[2]

---

[1] *Jamiʻ at-Tirmidhī* 1352.
[2] *Ṣaḥīḥ al-Bukhārī* 5151.

Second Research: Marriage

First Discussion: If Only One Person Has an Infectious Disease

Marriage is a blessing from the favors of Allāh (ﷻ) upon His slaves. It contains rest and tranquility, ease and reassurance, happiness and pleasure. It unites two individuals who start their lives by building a beautiful and calm nest that carries with it a beautiful future of enjoying marriage, having children, and fulfilling the responsibilities that Islām requires of them regarding the home.

Therefore, if the goal of marriage is noble, then honesty and clarity are required at the beginning of the bond between the bride and groom. This is based upon the statement of Allāh (ﷻ):

﴿ يَا أَيُّهَا الَّذِينَ آمَنُوا اتَّقُوا اللَّهَ وَكُونُوا مَعَ الصَّادِقِينَ ﴿١١٩﴾ ﴾

O you who believe, be afraid of Allāh, and be with those who are truthful.[1]

And the statement of the Prophet (ﷺ):

إِنَّ الصِّدْقَ يَهْدِي إِلَى الْبِرِّ، وَإِنَّ الْبِرَّ يَهْدِي إِلَى الْجَنَّةِ، وَإِنَّ الرَّجُلَ لَيَصْدُقُ حَتَّى يَكُونَ صِدِّيقًا، وَإِنَّ الْكَذِبَ يَهْدِي إِلَى الْفُجُورِ، وَإِنَّ الْفُجُورَ يَهْدِي إِلَى النَّارِ، وَإِنَّ الرَّجُلَ لَيَكْذِبُ، حَتَّى يُكْتَبَ عِنْدَ اللَّهِ كَذَّابًا

Truthfulness leads to righteousness, and righteousness leads to Paradise. And a man keeps on telling the truth until he becomes a truthful person. Falsehood leads to wickedness, and wickedness leads to the Hellfire, and a man may keep on telling lies until he is written with Allāh as a liar.[2]

When the suitor proposes to someone who he wants to marry, he must be clear with her about the diseases or illnesses that he suffers from. He must be frank about this because she will be with him after marriage, and the same applies to her.

When the suitor presents himself for marriage to his fiancée and has an infectious or a genetic disease that will negatively impact their lives, if he does not clarify this until after the marriage he places himself and his healthy wife in a very difficult predicament. This is considered deception and fraud. The Prophet (ﷺ) warned

---

[1] Sūrah at-Tawbah 9:119.

[2] *Ṣaḥīḥ al-Bukhārī* 6094.

against deception, and explained that those who deceive are not upon his guidance or his *sunnah*. He said:

مَنْ غَشَّ فَلَيْسَ مني

Whoever deceives (people) does not belong to me.[1]

This will negatively affect their lives, and the discord will increase between them because the spouse was not sincere in explaining his condition before marriage.

The pure *sharī'ah* forbids the individual from harming himself. Allāh (ﷻ) said:

﴿ وَلَا تُلْقُوا بِأَيْدِيكُمْ إِلَى التَّهْلُكَةِ ١٩٥ ﴾

And do not throw yourselves into destruction.[2]

When the healthy person is surprised by this situation and they realized they married a sick person who suffers great harm, the impact on their life will always remain. The pure *sharī'ah* forbids the individual from harming himself and from harming others. The Prophet (ﷺ) said:

لاَ ضَرَرَ وَلاَ ضِرَارَ

---

[1] *Ṣaḥīḥ Muslim* 102.
[2] Sūrah al-Baqarah 2:195.

There should be neither harming nor reciprocating harm.[1]

It is obligatory upon the sick party to inform the healthy party of their condition before the marriage contract, so the healthy party can make an informed decision. At this point, they will either decide to continue on with the marriage or distance themselves away from this marriage in order to protect themselves from harm. The Prophet (ﷺ) directed one of his companions when he married a woman from the 'Anṣār. When the man informed him that he had not seen her, he said:

فَانْظُرْ إِلَيْهَا فَإِنَّ فِي أَعْيُنِ الأَنْصَارِ شَيْئًا

Then look at her, for there is something in the eyes of the 'Anṣār.[2] **(Meaning that some of them have features which cause aversion.)**

This instruction was concerning something that someone may not care about or give much importance to. However, the Messenger of Allāh (ﷺ) wanted to show the necessity of being upon clarity about a potential spouse. This is so that after marriage no one is surprised by something that will have a negative impact upon their life.

---

[1] *Sunān Ibn Mājah* 2341.

[2] *Mishkāt al-Maṣābīḥ* 3098.

So how much more so if the disease carried by either the groom or the bride is an infectious disease that will result in harming the healthy spouse and the offspring that come from them?!

Based on that, it is not permissible for someone who proposes marriage to conceal having an infectious or hereditary disease that will affect their spouse. He must clarify his condition and take the necessary preventive measures to avoid harm to the healthy person.

Second Discussion: If Both People Have an Infectious Disease

If the suitor proposes to marry a woman, and they explain to each other that they are carrying an infectious or genetic disease that is harmful to them and their offspring—and they agree to this—they must return this matter to the doctors who are familiar with these specific diseases and seek their advice concerning this affair.

First: The Medical Standpoint

It is known that passing judgment on something is dependent on having a proper understanding of that thing. The degree of the disease that each suitor is carrying must be known. This will determine whether the two individuals are able to marry or not.

It is known that diseases, from a medical point of view, are divided into infectious and non- infectious diseases. Non-infectious diseases can be prevented from affecting the other person so that this does not affect them after marriage. Based upon that, marriage to someone with a non-infectious disease has no bearing. Therefore, if two people suffer from the same non-infectious disease, it has even less bearing upon the marriage.

However, if the diseases are infectious and the two suitors want to marry—while knowing of the other's condition and that they are afflicted with the same disease—then marriage between them is preferable due to its benefits and warding off evil. This is with the condition that both of them continue treatment.

Second: The Sharī'ah Standpoint

The scholars have two different statements concerning this matter.

First Viewpoint: Marriage Is Permissible

Marriage is permissible if doctors who specialize in these diseases acknowledge through a committee that these diseases predominantly have no negative impact on the marriage on both parties, and that the positives outweigh the negatives. In this case, the affected spouses can marry each other. The aim of preventing marriage is avoid a person sick with an infectious disease uniting with a healthy person and transmitting the infection to them. So if the spouses are infected with the same disease, even if it is contagious, the prohibition from marriage is removed.

If the spouses can be treated from these diseases before marriage, and vaccinated with appropriate treatment, then this is better and more appropriate. If the disease has no cure, there is no problem if they get married, provided both parties agree. But still, this marriage does not take place except after taking the opinion of specialists from the medical point of view. This is in order to know the impact of this marriage on the two parties, as well as its effect on their lives and the resulting offspring.

Those who say that it is permissible have used some rational evidence. This includes saying that each of them suffers from the same disease or close to it, and that both of them will bear this calamity as long as they share it. So because of this, there is no need to shelter them from each other. This does not involve injustice, harm, or deception. The matter between them is clear and both spouses bear the consequences of that as long as they agree to marry.

The fact that they are living together, enjoying the marital life, and not falling into the forbidden is better for them and the society around them. Otherwise, their disease could spread into society by way of impermissible actions.

Second Viewpoint: Marriage Is Impermissible

Medical professionals who deal with these diseases are aware of the impact they have on the individual and society. Therefore, if they know that each of these people carries a disease different from the other, and that these diseases cause a deterioration in their health and that their harm is real, then we look to see if the harms outweigh the benefits. We also look at their desire and urgency to get married. If the situation is such that if they are prevented from getting married they will fulfill their desires in an impermissible way, and thus spread their disease and cause harm to the society, then it is better for them to marry each other. But if the harms in not getting married are less than the benefits, then it is better if they do not get married. This is taken from the *sharī'ah* principle "warding off harm takes precedence over attaining benefit." This principle is used for these two individuals. It varies according to the person and the severity of disease in terms of the infection and their genetics.

This matter must be referred to the specialists who can direct them to what is best. They must be deliberate, taking their time to consider the consequences and the pros and cons. Medical professionals must advise them to do what is best for them, and they must give them advice that will not harm the greater society.

They must look at the benefits and harms, as we previously mentioned. If the harms are greater, it is best not to marry. If the benefits are greater, it is best to marry. These diseases may go away with treatment. In this case, there are no negative aspects. Or if there are some negative aspects, they are less than the benefits for the individuals and society as a whole.

The following was mentioned in the synopsis of the seventh gathering of the Islāmic Organization for Medical Sciences in

Kuwait regarding infectious diseases; especially AIDS.[1] "Two infected people can have sexual intercourse, preferably using male or female condoms to prevent the repeated transmission of infection between them. It's possible for the virus to mutate inside the body of an infected person, and it can also mutate due to repeated transmission of the disease between two infected people."[2]

If regulations are put in place for the infected spouses when they cohabitate, and they adhere to these regulations, it is beneficial for them and society.

The regulations are as follows:

1. They should use some type of modern medical technology that prevent infection, especially in the case of dangerous diseases such as AIDS.
2. They should continue treatment and follow up with their specialists, so there will be a desire to find a cure from these diseases or at least weaken the effect they have upon the person.
3. They should try to avoid conceiving children, especially AIDS patients. As for other diseases, they must look at this from a medical point of view. If the fetus will not be affected, it is permissible for them to conceive while putting certain safety measures in place to protect the fetus from

---

[1] Translator's note: Acquired Immunodeficiency Syndrome.

[2] Dr. Aḥmad Rajā'ī al-Jundī.

these diseases. If the fetus will be affected, it is best not to conceive children to ensure the children are not afflicted with the same disease or something that will cause them to be mentally or physically disabled.

Third Research: Intimacy

First Discussion: Intimacy Without Intercourse

If the man and woman desire to consummate the marriage, and one of them has an infectious disease while the other spouse is healthy, they must refer to some directives relating to their situation. If the spouses wish to enjoy each other without intercourse, is this considered a danger to the healthy spouse if they enjoy each other through kissing, touching, and exchanging salvia?

In this case, it is necessary to return to the competent authority for the medical point of view to see whether these methods are considered to be contagious or not.

Doctors are divided into three groups surrounding this issue.

First group: This group believes that living together, intermingling, and even intimacy does not spread disease. Rather, it is only spread by a limited number of means which they have clarified.

Some of these means are sexual intercourse through fornication or homosexuality. It is also spread through blood transfer by way of sharing needles and syringes, organ transplants, cupping, shaving, and other means where blood is transferred.

Infectious disease can also be transferred by sharing drug needles used by an infected person. And the disease is transmitted through the fetus in the mother's womb when she is pregnant, or during childbirth or breastfeeding.

As for kissing and touching, the disease is not transmitted by way of this because its presence in saliva is extremely minute. One study suggests HIV is not transmitted through saliva, sweat, tears, urine, breath, shaking hands, pool water, public restrooms, toilets, food, or drinking water.[1]

Second group: This group believes it is possible that infectious diseases can be transmitted through saliva because human T cell, also called T lymphocyte, is sometimes present in saliva. Researchers have been able to extract it from the saliva of AIDS patients and people in contact with the same disease, in the role of a precursor (a precursor is a compound that participates in a chemical reaction that produces another compound.) This supports the theory that the infectious virus agents can be transmitted by kissing or by

---

[1] Refat Kamal, *The Story of AIDS*, 91.

means of droplets that fly from the mouth into the air when sneezing and coughing.

Third group: This group believes unprotected oral sexual intercourse carries some risks of infection with HIV, but the available data so far are very limited and does not give an accurate determination of the degree of risk that may arise from this type of sexual relationship. Saliva contains very little HIV, and kissing has not yet been shown to cause disease transmission. However, if there is bleeding from the gums or mouth sores, there are theoretical risks of HIV transmission during a deep or wet kiss.[1]

Some of them believe that the disease has spread to dozens of innocent children whose parents contracted AIDS, and the infection of these children was the result of close contact between the mother and her newborn.[2]

Conclusion of the medical viewpoint: This disease is not transmitted without sexual intercourse. It is not transmitted by kissing. However, there is a theory that the disease may be transmitted by this, and it is supported by the findings of the researchers who extracted the virus from saliva.

---

[1] Dr. 'Alī Nimah.

[2] Dr. Muḥammad al-Bar.

Second Discussion: Utilizing Protection During Intimacy

Definition of condom:

It is a sterile rubbery plastic membrane that is placed on the penis to prevent contact between secretions of the two parties. Its purpose it to continue marital life without physical disturbances, and to a large extent prevent disease from spreading to the healthy spouse.

The Medical Community's Opinion on the Use of Condoms

It is medically known that sexual intercourse is the most conducive means for transmitting infectious diseases from a sick person to a healthy person. If direct sexual contact takes place between a person with an infectious disease and a healthy person, the healthy person will be in great danger as this is a cause of transmitting the disease to them.

Doctor Muḥammad Sadiq stated, "A woman married to a man with the AIDS virus must refrain from having sexual intercourse with him. This disease is a threat to her, and a threat to the fetus that will be created later.[1]

He also said, "Because the fluid contained in semen carries the virus, if a spouse infected with the virus has sexual intercourse

---

[1] Dr. Muhammad Sadiq, *AIDS: Medicine's Great Dilemma*, 352.

with their healthy spouse, the healthy spouse will become infected in most cases. Therefore, women who were married to men carrying the virus became carriers of the virus more times than not."[1]

A study on the transmission of the AIDS virus reported, "The husband transmitting AIDS to his healthy wife is possible, especially if he refuses to use a condom."[2]

Question: What is the result of using a condom?

Answer: The use of a professional grade condom reduces the risk of transmissing the disease to a low probability, if the type of condom is high quality and used properly.

In the case where one of the spouses is infected, doctors advise them to avoid sexual intercourse as much as possible. If they insist on having sexual relations, they should utilize a condom to prevent their sexual fluids from mixing. This will reduce the probability of transmitting the disease from the sick person to the healthy person. However, the possibility exists that the condom may rupture. Therefore, safety is not guaranteed but it provides safety to a large extent.[3]

---

[1] Dr. Muḥammad Bar, *AIDS: The Plague of Our Generation*, 70.

[2] Dr. Muḥammad Haythm, *The Islamic Vision for the Communal Problem of AIDS.*

[3] Refat Kamal, *The Story of AIDS.*

When a condom is used correctly, the chance of transmitting a disease is reduced to seven percent.

Difference Between Using and Not Using a Condom

If a condom is not used:

This matter varies according to the person infected and the type of infection. It has been medically proven that infection is transmitted from an infected man to a healthy woman at a rate of one in one thousand per sexual encounter. From an infected woman to a healthy man, the rate of transmission is one in two thousand per sexual encounter. The percentage may exceed this limit when there are other factors as clarified by doctors, such as infection with other infectious diseases, sexual intercourse during the woman's menstrual or postpartum period, or when bleeding occurs during the sexual encounter for other reasons such as breaking the hymen or rape.

If a condom is used:

Based upon one study of 15,000 sexual encounters between married couples, if a condom is always used, and used correctly, the percentage resulted in zero cases of transfer.

The Jurists' Opinion on the Use of Condoms

If we examine the reality of those who are infected with diseases, we find that the soul naturally flees from every infectious disease. So, what if these diseases are transmitted by way of cohabiting with the spouse, sleeping next to them, and intimacy with them? From the mercy of Allāh (ﷻ) is that He made the marital life differ completely from the animalistic life experienced by the people of perversion and whims. Marriage is a family bond. Intrinsic compassion is rooted within the hearts of the husband and wife. Because medical specialists consider the means of transmitting disease to be limited, the healthy spouse may choose to stay with the sick spouse despite the adversity of this disease, especially if the wife is the healthy spouse. Although she is terrified of these incurable diseases that naturally cause fear and confusion, she also fears being categorized as a "spinster." This is a term used to refer an unmarried woman who is older than what is perceived as the prime age range during which women usually marry. Her grief increases when she fears separation or that her children may be raised as orphans. Despite these circumstances and bitter reality, the healthy wife may also prefer to safeguard herself and choose the lesser of two harms, thus choosing not to place herself in harms way.

Based on this medical opinion, there are two scholarly opinions in this case.

First Opinion: Intimacy Without Intercourse

The first opinion is that intimacy without intercourse is forbidden, and thus it is permissible for the healthy spouse to request marital separation. They use as proof the statement of Allāh (ﷻ):

﴿ وَلَا تُلْقُوا بِأَيْدِيكُمْ إِلَى التَّهْلُكَةِ ﴿١٩٥﴾ ﴾

And do not throw yourselves into destruction.[1]

This is a general principle in which Allāh (ﷻ) forbids the people from placing themselves in harm's way or throwing themselves into destruction. The explanation of this verse states this is to leave off something good in preference of something of lesser value which eventually leads to destruction, such as not spending your wealth that results in death.[2]

In this case, it involves leaving off health and going toward sickness. The Prophet (ﷺ) warned us against harming ourselves or others. He said:

لاَ ضَرَرَ وَ لاَ ضِرَارَ

There should be neither harming nor reciprocating harm.[3]

This matter, undoubtably, is from the greatest harms because the person is intentionally causing harm to themselves. This position taken by the Prophet (ﷺ) shows that it is permissible in the *sharī'ah* to adopt means to ward off harm. When a delegation from the tribe of Thaqīf arrived to give their pledge of allegiance to

---

[1] Sūrah al-Baqarah 2:195.

[2] *Tafsīr ibn Kathīr*.

[3] *Sunān Ibn Mājah* 2341.

the Prophet (ﷺ), there was a man with leprosy among them. He said to them:

إِنَّا قَدْ بَايَعْنَاكَ فَارْجِعْ

We have accepted your allegiance, so you may go.[1]

It is known that infectious diseases, especially AIDS, require distance and separation from those affected in order to ward off harm. Therefore, intimacy is not permissible between a healthy spouse and a spouse with an infectious disease, even if there is no intercourse.

Second Opinion: Intimacy Without Direct Contact with the Vagina

The second opinion is that intimacy without direct contact with the vagina is permissible, but they should still utilize protection such as condoms. Those with this opinion use as evidence that the basic principle is that the marriage should remain stable and separation should not take place. Thus, once the marriage is confirmed as valid, it should not be separated except by way of proof from the Qur'ān and *sunnah*.

---

[1] Ṣaḥīḥ Muslim 2231.

Ibn Hazm (ﷺ) said, "Once a marriage is valid, it is not annulled by way of leprosy, albinism, nor insanity, or upon finding faults with the spouse.[1]

In addition to this, spreading the disease without direct contact with the vagina is doubtful, and certainty is not removed because of doubt. Rather, doubt is secondary to certainty, and the certainty is that the marriage remains intact. Also, preventive measures should be limited to the pathways of disease transmission. And as long as this direct transmission is not a carrier, what is the need to prohibit it?

There is a known principle that states, "Something done out of necessity can only be done according to the minimal extent required." This is a basic principle that is relevant in this case. This is the principle. So, if the disease is not transmitted by way of intimacy outside of sexual intercourse, then what is the reason to prohibited it? If this is the case, then depriving the husband of his wife is a physical and psychological punishment in addition to the psychological and health pain he is already suffering.

An AIDS patient who was fired from his job said, "As an AIDS patient, you are not only suffering from AIDS, but living as an outcast in society. Even when you die, they refuse to prepare

---

[1] *Al-Muḥallā* 10/63.

your body, and nothing makes you feel more miserable than this."[1]

Among those scholars who believe the marital life should continue in this case, it is understood from their speech that they permit sexual intercourse between the spouses. Therefore, intimacy without intercourse is more rightfully permitted.

In the "Islāmic Jurisprudence Study of Preventive Measures from Spreading AIDS" it says, "If the disease is one that can be spread, then the spouses have a choice to continue with the marriage or to separate. But I lean toward the necessity to continue in the marriage. We should consider the human element in this situation and continue until Allāh (ﷻ) decrees their affair."[2]

Based on that, the one who contemplates the two previous sayings finds that both of them should work to preserve the marriage, and the basic principle is respecting the pact of marriage and marital life. But when the danger remains clear to doctors, or there is an strong possibility of disease transmission, then prevention is the right thing.

Based upon that, if you ponder both opinions, we see that both opinions deserved to be implemented. The basis is to respect the contract of marriage and the marital life. But when danger is clear

---

[1] Dr. Muḥammad Bar, *AIDS: The Plague of Our Generation*," 79.

[2] Dr. Aḥmad Mūsā.

according to doctors, and there is a strong possibility of transmitting the disease, then prevention is the best thing.

The marriage is permissible whenever it becomes evident to the specialists that the disease is less likely to be transmitted through saliva and intimate cohabitation excluding sexual intercourse. Intimacy is permissible if there is no direct contact between the private areas if the following guidelines are applicable.

1. The possibility of transmitting infection is very low.

2. The spouses are committed to using all precautions recommended by the doctor, including the use of condoms regularly and accurately.

3. They must continue to use condoms, even if this lasts for a prolonged period of time, and they cannot become lenient in this matter or abandon them because the marriage is intended to remain intact.

If these preventive measures are not in place, it is preferred to prevent intimacy because this is safer, especially for the more serious diseases such as AIDS.

The doctor will investigate the particular situation of the couple if it is believed using a condom is practical for the spouses, and they will be disciplined in using it, and they are aware of the danger of leaving it, and the doctor knows the infection rate is minimal. If the couple is young and undisciplined, with strong desires, it is best to prevent them from marrying because their lust will overtake them, and the healthy spouse will become infected by the sick spouse.

If the spouses are mature and rationale, the correct position is they are permitted to have sexual intercourse because they are more disciplined, able to control their desires, and less likely to abandon the use of condoms during intercourse.

Fourth Research: Pregnancy

The family is the small community in which a small child is born and raised from an early age, from the beginning of their life, in the care of their family. The child is imprinted with its character and specific traits which are recognized by what they incline to, what they like, and what they dislike. For this reason, the sociologists acknowledge the home as the first fountain that supplies the nation with men and women. If this spring is good, pure, and free from corrupting impurities, its supply will be good for the Muslim nation. This community will produce strong young women and virtuous preachers. And if this spring is tainted with impurities and is based on chaos and neglect, then it will be evil for the ummah, a threat to its foundation.

Allāh (ﷻ) spoke the truth, He said:

﴿وَالْبَلَدُ الطَّيِّبُ يَخْرُجُ نَبَاتُهُ بِإِذْنِ رَبِّهِۦ وَالَّذِي خَبُثَ لَا يَخْرُجُ

إِلَّا نَكِدًا ﴿٥٨﴾﴾

And the good land - its vegetation emerges by the permission of its Lord; but that which is bad - nothing emerges except sparsely, with difficulty.[1]

If he selects a righteous woman free from diseases and illness, they will produce healthy offspring with the permission of Allāh (ﷻ). The family will benefit, as well as the community. With this, the importance of offspring to humanity becomes clear to us. Having offspring is the means to the longevity of mankind. If a couple is able to conceive but they delay having children for specific reasons, they will face embarrassment as time goes by. Therefore, the use of contraception should be limited to special circumstances, and there should be a desire to have children. But if the specialists have a ponderance of evidence that a child conceived by this couple will have a life of illness and hardship, they must look to decide whether it is better to have children or not. Here we point to the importance of the medical opinion in this matter, so the appropriate religious opinion can be made upon clear evidence.

---

[1] Sūrah al-'A'rāf 7:58.

Medical Opinion

Doctors have determined that pregnancy is one of the reasons for the transmission of an infectious disease from mother to fetus. Doctor Muḥammad Bar and Doctor Muḥammad Safa both said, "In addition to children who contract AIDS as a result of blood transfusions or due to contaminated haemophilia[1] blood products, there are a number of children who develop AIDS as a result of transmission of the virus from one of the parents to the child."[2]

They also said, "The virus is also transmitted to the embryos and infects them, and there are several theories about how the virus reaches the embryos.

1. Infected sperm: Infection occurs at an early stage, and some miscarriages are due to this reason.

2. From the mother's blood to the fetus's blood by way of the placenta, from there to the umbilical cord and then to the fetus.

3. During childbirth as the child descends from the uterus into an infected vagina.

---

[1] Translator's note: Haemophilia is a mostly inherited genetic disorder that impairs the body's ability to make blood clots, a process needed to stop bleeding. As a result, patients suffering from this require regular blood transfusions.

[2] Dr. Muḥammad Bar, *AIDS: The Plague of Our Generation*," 80.

4. After childbirth because of the intimate connection between the child and the affected mother or father, often before symptoms appear.

5. During in vitro fertilization (IVF), and several cases have already occurred in Australia.[1]

Doctor Muḥammad Sadiq said, "Pregnant women are more susceptible to disease because the changes that occur to their immune system during pregnancy greatly increase the change of infection."[2]

Using the latest method for detecting viruses, some doctors stated that the infection rate of the fetus while inside the womb is a small percentage that does not exceed ten percent. Most infection to the fetus occurs during childbirth as a result of contamination due to contact between the fetus and infected genital secretions. This occurs at a rate of 30%. In 60% of cases, the infection is not transmitted directly from the mother to the fetus.

Some doctors say that ten percent of infections occur during pregnancy, while 20-30% of infections occur during childbirth because secretions carry germs.

It is evident from the above that children get infected by way of their infected mother during pregnancy and childbirth.

---

[1] Dr. Muḥammad Bar, *AIDS: The Plague of Our Generation*," 72.
[2] Dr. Muḥammad Bar, *AIDS: The Plague of Our Generation*," 347.

Pregnancy sometimes leads to death of the infected mother. Although it is not a direct cause of her death, it worsens the disease in the mother and this leads to her death. Consequently, she dies while leaving behind children who have the same disease.

Effective Treatment for an Infected Mother During Pregnancy

Through medical research by specialists, it became clear to them that there are three options for the pregnant mother with an infectious disease.

1. She becomes pregnant while suffering from an infectious disease, then gives birth naturally, breastfeeds her newborn, and does not use anti-virus treatment. In this case, the infection rate is 13-45% if she has a natural birth and breastfeeds.

2. If the affected mother becomes pregnant, does not use treatment, then gives birth by cesarean section, the infection rate drops to almost half the previous rate.

3. The infected mother becomes pregnant and uses effective treatment, such that the amount of virus in the blood is lower than the minimum of less than two percent. And it is the same whether the birth is natural or by cesarean section, and if she does not breastfeed. Some say the rate of infection for this circumstance is eight percent or less. And

it is clear that this method reduces the infection rate of the fetus.

The Sharī'ah Opinion

Viewpoint Against Pregnancy

One viewpoint is that the woman suffering from an infectious disease—whatever type it may be—should be advised to take the necessary precautions to avoid pregnancy and childbearing. This is not to cut off her lineage and offspring, nor to prevent her from fulfilling her motherly desire to have a child. Rather, the reason is due to the problems and harms that result from this type of pregnancy.

Problems that may arise:

First: The AIDS virus, or other dangerous infectious diseases, are transmitted from an infected mother to her fetus through the means mentioned by the medical community. These means are as follows.

1. Through the placenta during pregnancy, and this occurs at about ten percent

2. During childbirth, and this occurs over 30% of the time

3. During breastfeeding and close contact

Second: The woman has natural physical weakness, and these weaknesses increase when she gets pregnant.

﴿ حَمَلَتْهُ أُمُّهُ وَهْنًا عَلَىٰ وَهْنٍ ﴿١٤﴾ ﴾

His mother bore him in weakness and hardship upon weakness and hardship.[1]

This weaken occurs to her when she is healthy and free of disease, so how much more so if she has a dangerous illness! She will experience hardship from all angles. So, for this reason she should avoid pregnancy if she has a serious disease like AIDS.

Third: The mother will combine two griefs. Her grief due to her own condition and the grief for her child that she passes the disease to. If, for the sake of argument, we say her child does not contract the disease, the pregnancy will still be difficult upon her.

Fourth: The mother's inability to care for her child if her disease becomes more severe.

Fifth: The chance of the fetus being infected with the disease of its mother is highly probable, not imaginary. In *sharī'ah* rulings, if there is an overwhelming chance that something might occur, it takes the ruling of something that will occur.

Sixth: The mother will be responsible for burdening her child with a terminal illness and causing it grief.

---

[1] Sūrah Luqmān 31:14.

Seventh: A patient with an infectious disease—especially AIDS—requires a great deal of money and time.

Eighth: The *sharīʿah* principles are put in place to repel harms. When a matter contains both harm and benefit, but the harm outweighs the benefit—as in the case of a woman with AIDS conceiving a child—the warding off a harm takes precedence over gaining a benefit.

Ninth: Pregnancy is from the factors that shorten the dormant stage of diseases. Rather, it accelerates the appearance of the disease. Thus, if the person suffers from an incurable disease, their health will deteriorate rapidly.

Ten: The impact of numerous infected children who have lost their mothers; the woman becomes pregnant and either passes the disease to her child, or she dies and her child becomes an orphan. Either way this is a hardship.

Viewpoint Allowing Pregnancy

Despite the strength of this opinion, it was before medicines were obtained to treat most infectious diseases. Thus, new factors have emerged to combat these diseases, such that effective treatment can reduce the rate of infection to less than eight percent, as previously mentioned. Based upon this conclusion from medical specialists and the small percentage rate of the fetus being infected by the mother, my viewpoint is that it is permissible for an infected woman to conceive a child if the following guidelines are in place.

1. The woman desiring to become pregnant uses regular treatment.
2. The woman must follow up with a specialist regularly regarding the proper use of her treatment and the virus's response to the treatment.
3. The woman's disease should be in its early stages, or her doctor must authorize and advise pregnancy at that stage of her disease.
4. She must follow up with the doctor and accept his recommendations when she wants to become pregnant.
5. There must be an overwhelming belief that the fetus will not be affected by the disease.

If the wife is healthy and the husband is infected with the disease, and they desire to remain together and conceive a child, the doctors have a say in this so the child can remain healthy and safe. This can be accomplished by separating the spermatozoa from the semen by a medical procedure known as sperm washing. The male's sperm is separated from the semen and the woman is artificially inseminated. With this procedure, the woman and their child will be healthy insha'Allāh.

Two hundred pregnancies were conceived this way and the children were all virus free. Neither the mother nor the child was infected. This method was successful because the virus is not found in the sperm. It is found in the semen.

Fifth Research: Aborting Pregnancy

This topic has three discussions.

First: Abortion of a fetus before 40 days

Second: Abortion of a fetus after 40 days, but before the soul is breathed into it

Third: Abortion of a fetus after the soul is breathed into it

Translator's addendum: The soul is breathed into the fetus after 120 days, also calculated as 17 weeks or 4 months. Shaykh ibn Baz said: "It is only called a child after four months, after the soul is breathed into it, and in the event of miscarriage or abortion, it must be washed and the funeral prayer offered for it. It is considered to be a child, and we hope that he will intercede for his parents." End quote from *Fataawa Noor 'ala ad-Darb* by Ibn Baz (13/482). **End of translator's addendum.**

First Discussion: Abortion of a Fetus Before 40 Days

Definition of abortion: Linguistically the term abortion is applied to two circumstances. It applies to the incomplete development of the fetus due to it dying before its completed term, whether by the action of the woman or involuntary.

The religious definition of abortion does not differ much from the linguistic meaning. It is often used as a synonym for the word stillborn and miscarriage.

Medically speaking, abortion is defined as the deliberate termination of the pregnancy inside the womb before it was able to live by itself, and that is before the 22nd week or before it reached a weight of 500 grams or more. Dr. Muḥammad Bar defined abortion as "terminating the fetus from inside the womb before the 28th week of pregnancy. And the weeks are counted starting from the last menstrual period." Dr. Philippe Landreau defined abortion as "terminating the fetus before the 28th week of pregnancy."

The Blessing of Children

Indeed, Allāh (ﷻ) bestowed His favor upon His slaves with the blessing of offspring, and He made it from the most noble and greatest blessing. Allāh (ﷻ) said:

﴿ الْمَالُ وَالْبَنُونَ زِينَةُ الْحَيَاةِ الدُّنْيَا ﴿٤٦﴾ ﴾

Wealth and children are the adornment of the life of this world.[1]

By way of offspring life continues on in this simple manner. The offspring are those who will populate the earth and assume authority after their fathers. They are the strength of the future. The Prophet (ﷺ) said:

إِذَا مَاتَ الإِنْسَانُ انْقَطَعَ عَمَلُهُ إِلاَّ مِنْ ثَلاَثَةٍ مِنْ صَدَقَةٍ جَارِيَةٍ وَعِلْمٍ يُنْتَفَعُ بِهِ وَوَلَدٍ صَالِحٍ يَدْعُو لَهُ

When the person dies, all his actions come to an end except for three; an ongoing charity, beneficial knowledge, and a righteous child who supplicates for him.[2]

Islām gives great importance to increasing the lineage and offspring and giving these offspring a sound upbringing based upon love of Allāh (ﷻ), His Messenger (ﷺ), and the believers. And it is based upon raising them to love doing good for those around them.

The Messenger of Allāh (ﷺ) said:

تَزَوَّجُوا الْوَدُودَ الْوَلُودَ إِنِّي مُكَاثِرٌ بِكُمُ الأَنْبِيَاءَ يَوْمَ الْقِيَامَةِ

---

[1] Sūrah al-Kahf 18:46.

[2] *Sunān an-Nasā'ī* 3651.

Marry the women who are loving and fertile, for indeed by way of you I shall have a greater number than the prophets on the Day of Judgment.[1]

Thus, they increase the *'ummah* of Muḥammad (ﷺ) by producing righteous offspring that will benefit Islām and the Muslims.

One of the things that appeared in later times was the emergence of abortions. They increased greatly and spread their impact on societies, especially western societies because of the moral decay they live in—the separation of families and being far away from family values. They practice adultery, homosexuality and the like, so infectious diseases spread among them. This affected the women and what they carry in their wombs. The world investigated the affair of abortion trying to decide if it was a healthy or unhealthy solution. As for the scholars, they have given *sharī'ah* rulings that clarify this matter.

Types of Abortions

Before knowing the opinions of the jurists regarding the ruling on abortion for women with an infectious disease, it is necessary to know the types of abortions that are widespread among people, doctors, and the jurists. This is because each group divided it into multiple categories according to different criteria.

---

[1] *Sunān an-Nasā'ī* 3227.

Abortions have been divided into three types.

1. Spontaneous abortions (miscarriages)
2. Therapeutic abortions
3. Social or criminal abortions

These categories are according to the motives and justifications given by the people.

Spontaneous Abortions, Also Known as Miscarriages

This happens without the women's will. The uterus works to expel the fetus that is not developing normally. This may happen because of a defect in the woman's reproductive system or because of an unforeseen mistake, such as carrying something heavy, stress, or drinking something harmful to the fetus. This is considered a natural abortion or miscarriage that occurred spontaneously without any outside intervention.

Therapeutic Abortion

This type of abortion is a medical necessity. This is when a doctor, who is trusted in his religion and knowledge, orders an abortion to save the life of the mother because she is in grave danger due to the pregnancy.

Social or Criminal Abortion:

This is to terminate the pregnancy in an illegal manner, by non-specialists, using various unconventional means to dispose of the fetus. It may also take place in medical clinics with the supervision of specialized doctors under the pretext of rescuing underage girls or women from unwanted pregnancies in exchange for large sums of money.

After this introduction, we will now explain the ruling on having an abortion before 40 days after conception.

Various opinions concerning abortion prior to forty days

Those Who Say It Is Permissible to Abort the Fetus Before 40 Days Without A Valid Reason

Some scholars from the Hanafī school of thought say it is permissible to abort the fetus before the soul is breathed into the fetus.[1]

Some scholars who following the Malikī and Shāfi'ī schools of thought say the fetus can be aborted before 40 days.[2] Other scholars from the Shāfi'ī school of thought say if the conception was by way of fornication, the fetus can be aborted before the soul is breathed into it.[3]

Some scholars from the Ḥanbalī school of thought say that in the early stages of pregnancy a woman is allowed to drink medicine that will remove the sperm drop but not the blood clot. They say if there is no soul, the soul will not be resurrected. So, what is

---

[1] *Fatḥ al-Taqdīr* 2/495.

[2] Explanation of Muwaṭṭā' of Imām Mālik.

[3] *Tuḥfat al-Ḥabib* 3/303.

understood from this is that they allow the abortion before the soul is breathed into the fetus.[1]

Those Who Say It Is Permissible to Abort the Fetus Before 40 Days With A Valid Reason

Some scholars from the Hanafī school of thought have said it is not permissible without a valid reason. They said, "If a person in a state of iḥrām for Ḥajj breaks an egg belonging to a bird, it is similar to hunting the bird during Ḥajj, and this is forbidden. So just as he is penalized for this, the woman who has an abortion without justification is also committing a sin.

Those Who Say It Is Hated to Abort the Fetus Before 40 Days

Some scholars state it is hated to abort the fetus whether there is a reason to do so or not. Some of the Hanafī scholars hold this opinion. They said it is hated to abort the fetus, even before the soul is breathed into, because once the sperm reaches the uterus its intended destination is towards life. Thus, it takes the ruling of a life just like the egg of a bird is sacred in the sacred land of Mecca during Hajj season.

---

[1] *Al-Furūq* 6/191.

Those Who Say It Is Impermissible to Abort the Fetus Before 40 Days

Some scholars say it is impermissible to abort the fetus before 40 days. This opinion has been narrated by some Malikī scholars who say it is impermissible to remove the sperm once it reaches the uterus.

Scholars from the Ḥanbalī and Shāfi‘ī schools of thought also say it is impermissible to abort the fetus, even before 40 days. This is the viewpoint of Ibn al-Jawzi and Ibn Aqīl.

Before clarifying the correct *sharī‘ah* opinion for aborting a fetus prior to 40 days, we shall look at what the medical professionals have said concerning this matter.

Medical doctors say abortion is allowable in the following circumstances.

1. If it is medically proven that the fetus will definitely contract the virus during the early stages of pregnancy, meaning the stages where an abortion is legislated
2. If it is in the interest of the mother because of the harm that pregnancy will inflict on her. In this case, they deemed abortion as justified to preserve the life of the mother.

It is clear that the virus, which is an infectious disease, arises during the early stages of pregnancy or during childbirth. Pregnancy is from the means by which infectious diseases, such as AIDS, are transmitted. So is it permissible to abort the fetus based solely on the strong possibility that the child might contract the AIDS virus?

Doctors have differed on this issue. In the book *AIDS: Medicine's Great Dilemma* it says, "It is better for a woman that has the AIDS virus to go for an abortion."

While most doctors say that if the pregnant woman can use drugs prescribed by a specialist that reduce the chance of infection to less than eight percent, it is best for her not to have an abortion.

The Correct Viewpoint Concerning Abortion Before 40 Days

From what is apparent, the most correct view is the opinion that it is not permissible to have an abortion prior to 40 days in the womb if there is not a valid Islāmic reason, even if it is prior to the soul being breathed into the fetus. The reasons for this are as follows. The sperm drop during its early stages of conception is referred to as a fetus. It is called such because the word fetus in the Arabic language stems from the word meaning that which is hidden, and the sperm drop is concealed in the womb of the mother. And in the Quran and pure *sunnah*, the fetus is respected and given consideration. Allāh (ﷻ) said:

﴿ يَا أَيُّهَا النَّاسُ إِن كُنتُمْ فِي رَيْبٍ مِّنَ الْبَعْثِ فَإِنَّا خَلَقْنَاكُم مِّن تُرَابٍ ثُمَّ مِن نُّطْفَةٍ ثُمَّ مِنْ عَلَقَةٍ ثُمَّ مِن مُّضْغَةٍ مُّخَلَّقَةٍ وَغَيْرِ مُخَلَّقَةٍ لِّنُبَيِّنَ لَكُمْ ﴿٥﴾ ﴾

O People, if you are in doubt about the Resurrection, then [consider that] indeed, We created you from dust, then from a sperm-drop, then from a clinging clot, and then from a lump of flesh, formed and unformed - that We may show you.[1]

And His statement:

﴿ وَلَقَدْ خَلَقْنَا الْإِنسَانَ مِن سُلَالَةٍ مِّن طِينٍ ﴿١٢﴾ ثُمَّ جَعَلْنَاهُ نُطْفَةً فِي قَرَارٍ مَّكِينٍ ﴿١٣﴾ ﴾

And certainly, did We create man from an extract of clay. Then We placed him as a sperm-drop in a firm lodging.[2]

---

[1] Sūrah Al-Ḥajj 22:5.

[2] Sūrah Al-Mu'minūn 23:12-13.

Ibn Kathir said[1] in his explanation of this verse, "The pronoun 'him' in the statement, 'Then We placed him as a sperm-drop' refers to mankind. Just as Allāh (ﷻ) said in another verse:

﴿ وَبَدَأَ خَلْقَ الْإِنسَانِ مِن طِينٍ ﴿٧﴾ ﴾

And He began the creation of man from clay.[2]

The Prophet (ﷺ) said:

إِنَّ خَلْقَ أَحَدِكُمْ يُجْمَعُ فِي بَطْنِ أُمِّهِ أَرْبَعِينَ لَيْلَةً

The creation of any one of you is collected in the womb of the mother for 40 nights.[3]

Some scholars have said that the sperm drop stage is the development stage, when the female sperm moves to the womb to unite for creation, and the gamete falls around the 14th day and settles in the womb after another seven days. It becomes a clot after another 19 days, that is 40 days after the first day of the last menstruation.

For this reason, this sperm drop has sanctity, and it is not permissible to remove it or harm it. Likewise, it is not permissible to remove it during the blood clot stage or lump of flesh stage, even

---

[1] *Tafsīr ibn Kathīr* 3/251.
[2] Sūrah as-Sajdah 32:7.
[3] *Ṣaḥīḥ Muslim* 2643.

if the soul has not yet been breathed into it. The exception is when there is a legitimate reason to do so. Otherwise, whoever performs the abortion is sinning, whether it is the doctor or someone who is unauthorized.

The Council of Senior Scholars issued the following statement, "It is not permissible to abort a pregnancy at any stage, unless there is a legitimate reason and within very precise limits. If the pregnancy is in the first stage, which is a period of 40 days, and aborting it serves a legitimate purpose or will ward off harm, it is permissible to abort it. But aborting it at this stage for fear of the difficulty of raising children or of being unable to bear the costs of maintaining and educating them, or for fear for their future, or because the couple feels that they have enough children – this is not permissible.[1]

Second Discussion: Abortion of A Fetus After 40 Days, Before the Soul Is Breathed Into It

We have clarified the opinion of the jurists and doctors about the issue of abortion before 40 days, and we have mentioned the disagreement of the jurists regarding that. It is clear from what was mentioned that the statement that it is impermissible is most correct, due to the evils contained therein. Here we will explain the

---

[1] Council of Senior Scholars, Fatwa 140.

ruling on abortion after 40 days, before the soul has been breathed into the fetus.

Scholars from the Malikī school of thought unanimously agree that abortion is unrestrictedly impermissible from the time the sperm drop enters the womb until the soul is breathed into it. This is on the basis that the sperm drop is ready to accept life. Thus, a crime against it is impermissible in every circumstance. Abortion of the fetus in its early stages infringes on its humanity and its right to life. This view was also stated by some of the Hanafī imāms, such as Imām al-Sarakhsī.[1]

As for the Ḥanbalīs, Shāfi'īs, and some Hanafīs, they are of the view that harming the fetus is from the stage of the embryo only, not before it, because before this stage it has not yet formed. As for the second stage of the embryo, even if a little forming appears it is more likely that abortion is not considered a crime at this stage. They say it is permissible to abort the fetus before the 42nd day, which is the stage when the fetus is between human existence and non-existence.

The contemporary scholars have two separate views on this matter. Some say it is permissible to abort the fetus before the first 120 days, meaning before the soul is breathed into it. Others say it is impermissible to abort the fetus once the sperm-drop enters the womb and attaches itself. The following was mentioned at the

---

[1] Translator's note: He died 483 years after the migration.

1983 symposium held in Kuwait on the topic of "Childbearing in the light of Islām," "The symposium reviewed the opinions of previous jurists and the sound consideration indicated by them ... the symposium became familiar with the data of contemporary medical scientific facts and concluded that the fetus is alive from the beginning of pregnancy. And that this life is respected, especially after the soul has been breathed in, and that it is not permissible to transgress against it except for extreme medical necessity."[1]

Doctor Jamīl ibn Mubārik said, "As for the issue of abortion—and Allāh knows best—it is only permissible if there is an extreme necessity for it. Otherwise, it is not permissible. This applies to before and after the creation of the fetus has begun, because to abort the fetus during the first stage of pregnancy is considered tampering and severing the path to pregnancy. Thus, other methods to avoid pregnancy should be used such as coitus interruptus and contraception."

Based on what was previously mentioned, the basic principle is that abortion is prohibited. Those who allowed it, only allow it in cases of necessity. The preservation of life is from the most important necessities. If it becomes certain that the fetus will be harmed by its mother, who is infected with an infectious disease such as AIDS, the permissibility of abortion is only after consulting

---

[1] *Childbearing in the Light of Islam*, 351.

reliable and trustworthy doctors, because there are doctors who are motivated by their love of money. They are willing to make money even at the expense of a sinless child.

The prohibition of abortion is even stronger if it appears the child will not be harmed by the mother's virus due to her using some of the previously mentioned safety measures, and so the transmission percentage is low. It is also known that some fetuses test positive in the early stages of pregnancy, then Allāh wills for the result to change to negative.

Third Discussion: Abortion of A Fetus After the Soul Is Breathed Into It

It is known that the soul is breathed into the fetus after 120 days. This has been affirmed in an authentic *ḥadīth* narrated by Ibn Masūd. The Messenger of Allāh (ﷺ) said:

إِنَّ أَحَدَكُمْ يُجْمَعُ خَلْقُهُ فِي بَطْنِ أُمِّهِ أَرْبَعِينَ يَوْمًا ثُمَّ يَكُونُ عَلَقَةً مِثْلَ ذَلِكَ ثُمَّ يَكُونُ مُضْغَةً مِثْلَ ذَلِكَ ثُمَّ يَبْعَثُ اللَّهُ مَلَكًا فَيُؤْمَرُ بِأَرْبَعِ كَلِمَاتٍ

The creation of any one of you is put together in his mother's womb for 40 days, then he becomes a piece of thick coagulated blood for a similar period. Then he becomes like a chewed piece of flesh for a similar period, then Allāh sends an angel who is enjoined to write down four things.[1]

---

[1] *Ṣaḥīḥ al-Bukhārī* 3208.

It is not known that there is a difference of opinion concerning the prohibition of abortion after the soul has been breathed into the fetus. Once the soul has been breathed into the fetus, there is a consensus that abortion is impermissible. It is considered murder, and there is no difference of opinion about this. The scholars who say abortion is impermissible after the soul has been breathed into the fetus say it does not matter if the life of the mother is in danger or not. They said, "If the fetus is alive and the mother's life will be in danger if the child remains alive, then it is not permissible to end the life of the child; because the thought that the mother might die is an assumption, and you cannot kill someone based upon an assumed outcome.

Based on that, the scholars have agreed that abortion is forbidden after the soul has been breathed in, except for a strong excuse such as if the fetus is a certain danger to the mother. This recommendation must come from reliable doctors, especially when the mother is affected with an infectious disease like AIDS and the disease is also a harm to the fetus.

Doctors have stated that an infectious disease such as AIDS usually does not harm the fetus, except after the pregnancy has progressed, the soul has been breathed into the fetus, or at birth. And therefore, abortion is not permissible in this case unless the confirmed danger to the mother is verified.

This topic was discussed in the jurisprudence council of the Muslim World League during the 12th session, which was held in

Mecca on Rajab 15-22, 1410 Hijri. It was stated that the Council decided by majority of votes the following: “If the pregnancy has reached 120 days, it is not permissible to abort it even if the medical diagnosis indicates that it is deformed, unless it is proven by the report of a medical committee of trusted, competent doctors that the pregnancy is a definite risk to the life of the mother. Then it is permissible to abort in an effort to ward off the greater of two harms.

And it was also issued by the Islāmic Fiqh Council in their “Resolution No. (90) (7/9)” regarding AIDS. and the jurisprudential rulings related to it, which states, “It is not permissible to abort the fetus of a mother with HIV infection, since the transmission of infection from a pregnant woman with AIDS to her fetus does not occur often until after the pregnancy progresses, the soul has been breathed into the fetus, or during childbirth.

Based on that, it is not permissible to abort the fetus of a woman with an infectious disease - such as AIDS because the soul has been breathed into it, and it is not permissible to kill it unlawfully. This is the opinion of the jurisprudential councils and health and Islāmic organizations, as previously mentioned.

Sixth Research: Sustainability of Marriage

First Discussion: Sustainability When Only One of the Spouses Has An Infectious Disease

Cohabitation in the language means to associate and to have social interaction with a friend, relative. Cohabitation with a woman is to have a wife and to live with her. The word meaning cohabitation is used to refer to the husband in the *ḥadīth* of the Messenger of Allāh (ﷺ). He said:

يَا مَعْشَرَ النِّسَاءِ تَصَدَّقْنَ، فَإِنِّي رَأَيْتُكُنَّ أَكْثَرَ أَهْلِ النَّارِ ". فَقُلْنَ وَبِمَ ذَلِكَ يَا رَسُولَ اللَّهِ قَالَ " تُكْثِرْنَ اللَّعْنَ وَتَكْفُرْنَ الْعَشِيرَ

"O women, give charity, for I have seen that you are the majority of the dwellers of Hell-Fire." The women asked, "What is the

reason for this O Messenger of Allāh?" He replied, "You curse frequently, and are ungrateful to your husbands."[1]

The technical terminology of cohabitation means what occurs between husband and wife such as affection and intimacy.

Living Together in Kindness

The *sharī'ah* incites married couples to live together in kindness. Allāh (ﷻ) said:

﴿ وَعَاشِرُوهُنَّ بِالْمَعْرُوفِ ﴿١٩﴾ ﴾

And live with them in kindness.[2]

And He (ﷻ) said:

﴿ وَلَهُنَّ مِثْلُ الَّذِي عَلَيْهِنَّ بِالْمَعْرُوفِ ﴿٢٢٨﴾ ﴾

And due to the wives is similar to what is expected of them, according to what is reasonable.[3]

'Abū Zayd said, "The men have to fear Allāh concerning the women just as the women have to fear Allāh concerning the men." Al-Ḍaḥāk said in the explanation of this verse, "If the woman obeys Allāh and obeys her husband, it is upon the man to

---

[1] *Ṣaḥīḥ al-Bukhārī* 1462.

[2] Sūrah an-Nisā' 4:19.

[3] Sūrah al-Baqarah 2:228.

have good companionship with her, avoid harming her, and spend upon her from his means.[1]

The Prophet (ﷺ) said:

اسْتَوْصُوا بِالنِّسَاءِ خَيْرًا فَإِنَّهُنَّ عِنْدَكُمْ عَوَانٍ

Treat the women kindly, because they are like captives in your hands.

The meaning of living with the wife in kindness, found in the command of Allāh (ﷻ), "and live with them in kindness,"[2] it is to give the wife her rights in full, along with having good etiquette and companionship with her.

Al-Jaṣṣās[3] said, "Treating her kindly is to give her all her rights, to include the dowry, spending upon her, and spending equal time with her if the husband has more than one wife. It is to avoid harming her with harsh speech, turning away from her or turning to others. It is to avoid frowning at her and striking her in the face."[4]

Good interaction between spouses is actualized by each one fulfilling the rights of the other and treating each other well with

---

[1] Ibn Qudāmah, *Al-Mughni.*

[2] Sūrah an-Nisā' 4:19.

[3] Translator's note: He was a Hanafi scholar from Bagdad. He died 370 years after the migration.

[4] Al-Jaṣṣās, *Rulings of the Qur'ān*, 2/132.

good companionship. Some rights are just for the wife, some are just for the husband, while some rights are shared. This is not the place to speak about the rights of the spouses, but I wanted to highlight this, to show the importance of the spouses being free from that which hinders an honorable marital life.

Question: Is it possible to sustain marital life between two spouses when one of them has an illness?

First, it is obligatory to know that if one of the spouses is afflicted with an illness it is obligatory upon them to inform the other party of the illness. We have already mentioned this in the second research, the ruling on marriage to someone with an infectious disease.

Second, if the healthy spouse is aware that the other spouse has an infectious disease, what is the ruling on them remaining together? This is what will be explained.

We have talked about the impact of an infectious disease on the life of an infected person, and the effect of that on those who interact with him, especially if he marries a healthy person.

This matter was previously mentioned by doctors and indicated that sexual contact between an infected person and a healthy person is considered one of the greatest means of transmitting disease. The rate of disease transmission through this reaches more than 90%; especially since there are certain sexual practices among those infected, such as sodomy, fornication, multiple sex partners, prostitution, and other means.

Therefore, doctors advise staying away from sexual intercourse as much as possible. If they insist on sexual intercourse, then they should utilize a male or female condom to prevent contact between the sexual secretions of both parties. This reduces the rate of infection to the healthy spouse.

It was stated in the study entitled "Researching Basic Information on AIDS" The possibilities of transmission from the sick spouse to the healthy spouse are possible, especially if the sick spouse refuses to use a condom.[1]

With regard to the later-day scholars, they differed concerning the ruling on sustaining a marriage if one spouse has an infectious disease. Some have said it is permissible for the healthy spouse to request a separation. And if the wife is healthy, it is not permissible for the sick husband to force his wife to remain with him or to force her to have sexual intercourse with him.

It is stated in the study entitled "Preventive Measures to Stop the Spread of AIDS in Light of the Islāmic Sharī'ah" that the healthy spouse has the right to refrain from sexual intercourse so they can remain safe from the disease. If the husband is healthy, he can request a divorce from his wife to protect himself, his future, and

---

[1] Muḥammad Khiyat, "Researching Basic Information on AIDS".

his future children from the possibility of infection by way of blood and breast milk.

If the disease is not infectious, the healthy person still has the right to separation, even if the healthy person does not want a separation.

If the wife is the healthy party, her guardians must take her by the hand and remove her from the marriage in order to implement the *sharī'ah* principle of preventing harm. If the husband is the healthy party, the Muslim *'ummah* must remove him and force him to separate from her if he does not do so on his own.

In a study pertaining to the *sharī'ah* rulings connected to AIDS, it states, "A healthy man should be prevented from marry a woman with a dangerous infectious disease such as AIDS more so than a foolish man should be prevented from squandering his money, because the foolish man squandering his life is more dangerous than him squandering his wealth."

But what is better, and the first thing that should be considered, is the condition of spouses as we mentioned in the second research. Thus, the possibility of preventing harm should be looked into; and this matter returns to the age of the spouses, their self-restraint, and their commitment to using safety measures to protect the healthy spouse from contracting the disease. This is what doctors consider weighing the benefits versus the harms. This is how the determination is made whether the spouses should remain together or separated.

Second Discussion: Sustainability When Both Spouses Have an Infectious Disease

If a man and a woman got married and it was found that they had the same infectious disease, whether that was before or after the marriage, due to falling into forbidden behavior, or through other means such as blood transfusion—and perhaps they were married for a long time and have had children—according to the *sharīʿah*, is it permissible for them to remain married? And if that is permissible, is there anything that should be observed according to the *sharīʿah*?

Medical professionals have not given conclusive advice as to whether or not spouses who both suffer from an infectious disease should remain together. Some of their statements suggested if they remain together their illnesses may worsen and increase the activity of the virus. However, there is no clear study that has followed up on such a case and demonstrated that with realistic examples.

It was mentioned in The Medical Symposium of the Islāmic Organization for Medical Sciences in Kuwait that what indicates some doctors believe that this has an effect, and that infection may be increase by sexual contact between the infected. They said that infected spouses can have intercourse with each other, and it is preferable to do so by using male or female condoms to prevent repeated transmission of infection between them, especially since the virus may change its quality inside the infected person's body and recurrence of mixing the infections causes the disease to mutate at a faster rate. This indicates the harm of perpetual sexual intercourse between two spouses who are both infected with an infectious disease.

However, some specialist doctors believe that marriage between two infected spouses is preferable and that the continuation of the cohabitation is better for them. This is because they are already infected with the disease, so the benefit of them remaining married is better than the expected evil that may occur if they are single. This is especially true if the virus responds to treatment on both sides.

As for the *sharī'ah* ruling, the scholars have ruled that each situation has its specific circumstance based on if the harm outweighs the benefit. If specialists determine the spouses will not be harmed, then there is no problem if they remain married.

Other scholars argue that it is obligatory that they remain together. Thus, it becomes clear from the words of doctors and scholars that two spouses suffering from an infectious disease should remain married unless doctors advise them to separate.

Seventh Research: Separation of Spouses

The scholars define a separation as dissolving the marriage by divorce or otherwise. The jurists have mentioned many reasons for the separation, and this is not the place to mention them. However, we will mention one of its causes which is related to our topic.

From the reasons for marriage separation is due to a defect. The consensus of scholars says a marriage separation is permissible due to a defect in either spouse, be it the man or the woman. Hanafī scholars singled out the permissibility of marriage separation if the defect exists within the husband.

Defects allowing the woman to request separation include the man missing a penis, if his penis is extremely small like a grain of rice, impotence, and castration. This is the viewpoint of 'Abū Hanifa and 'Abū Yūsūf.

Defects allowing the husband to request separation include the woman whose vagina is closed, blocked such that it prevents intercourse, or rectovaginal fistula which is an abnormal connection between the lower portion of the large intestine—the rectum—and the vagina, halitosis, or a bad odor from the vagina.

Shared defects allowing either spouse to request separation include insanity, leprosy, albinism, if the spouse defecates or urinates during sexual intercourse, and hermaphroditism. Scholars from the Ḥanbalī school of thought added bowel incontinence and urinary incontinence to the list. Also, runny sores in the vulva because this will cause the husband to avoid his wife. 'Abū al-Khaṭṭāb[1] said, "Excluded from this are fistula (an abnormal connection between generally two epithelial-lined vessels or organs) and hemorrhoids.

The aforementioned defects do not prove that the defects are limited to those mentioned. Ibn al-Qayyim said, "Limiting the defects to six, seven, or eight, —while omitting greater or equal defects—has no basis. Some people are repulsed by blindness, deafness, mutism, and amputation of hands or feet. The premise is that a defect is defined as everything that alienates the spouse and thus prevents the intent of marriage, which is affection and mercy. So in this case, the spouse is given the choice to remain or leave."[2]

---

[1] Died 540 years after the migration.

[2] *Zād al-Ma'ād.*

Conditions for Separation Due to Defect

The scholars differ concerning the conditions allowing marital separation due to defect. The viewpoints are as follows.

1. The spouse has the right to dissolve the marriage if they are not pleased with the defect before or after the marriage is consummated, during or after the marital contract, and whether they clearly state they are not pleased with the defect or they allude to it. If the healthy spouse is pleased with the defect and they are able to have intimacy, then no one has the right to dissolve their marriage after that. This is the viewpoint of those from the Ḥanbalī school of thought, and the scholars from the Shāfiʿī school of thought agree with them except in the case of erectile dysfunction. Some scholars hold the position that if the woman is pleased with his erectile dysfunction after consummation, then she does not have grounds to dissolve the marriage, while the Ḥanbalīs disagree with this position. Other scholars say even if the wife allows the husband to be intimate with her after she knows of his erectile dysfunction, this does not remove her right to dissolve the marriage.

Thus, the question becomes whether her approval of the man's defect before marriage removes her option to dissolve the marriage at a later date. For example, if he informed her of his erectile dysfunction and she approved of it directly or indirectly, the consensus of scholars is that this removes her option. Imām Shāfiʿī said the exception is in the case of erectile dysfunction because he may have erectile dysfunction in one marriage but not another, as his inability to have intercourse with one woman does not necessitate that he will not be able to have intercourse with another wife.

2. Does the spouse requesting annulment of the marriage due to defects have to be free of defects? The scholars have varied views on this issue. The Malikī scholars hold the view that if the spouse requesting a separation has the same defect as their spouse, in this case the husband has a right to request a separation because he gave her the dowry under the premise that she was free from this defect. But if they both have different defects, each spouse has the right to request a separation.

The Shāfi'ī scholars say the person with a defect has the right to request the annulment of the marriage for a defect whether his defect is the same type of defect or not.

The Ḥanbalī scholars say the person with a defect has the right to request a marriage annulment if their spouse suffers from a different defect. For example, if the man has leprosy and the woman is insane, both spouses have the right to request annulment because they both have valid reasons. Except in the case where a man who is castrated marries a woman whose vagina is blocked, then it is not proper that they should have the option to annul the marriage because their similar defects do not prevent them from enjoying each other.

Therefore, if both spouses have the same defect, one viewpoint says they do not have the option to request separation because they are equal. The other viewpoint says they have the right to request separation because the reason to request separation is present.

It was stated in a decision of the Islāmic Fiqh Council, 90 (7/9), in paragraph 5, emanating from the Organization of the Islāmic Conference in Jeddah, "The healthy spouse has the right to request a divorce from the spouse who is infected with HIV/AIDS. The wife has the right to request a divorce from her infected husband given that the Acquired Immunodeficiency Syndrome (AIDS) is an infectious disease that is transmitted mainly through sexual contact.

The proof that the healthy spouse can request a separation is taken from the following. Allāh (ﷻ) wants ease for His slave and He does not want difficulty for them. The Exalted said:

﴿ يُرِيدُ اللَّهُ بِكُمُ الْيُسْرَ وَلَا يُرِيدُ بِكُمُ الْعُسْرَ ﴿١٨٥﴾ ﴾

Allāh intends for you ease, and He does not want to make things difficult for you.[1]

[1] Sūrah al-Baqarah 2:185.

First Discussion: The Wife Who Does Not Have an Infectious Disease Requesting A Separation

A healthy wife remaining with a husband affected with an infectious disease will be a hardship upon her which she will not be able to bear. Also, the doctors have affirmed the danger of infectious diseases, especially AIDS, and the *sunnah* commands us to distance ourselves from disease. The Prophet (ﷺ) said:

وَفِرَّ مِنَ الْمَجْذُومِ كَمَا تَفِرُّ مِنَ الأَسَدِ

One should run away from the leper as one runs away from a lion.[1]

'Umar said to the man, "Did you inform her that you are sterile?" The man replied, "No." 'Umar said, "Inform her and give her the choice to stay or leave."[2]

This narration shows that childbearing is an important goal for some, and the inability to do so is considered a defect. For this reason, 'Umar (رضي الله عنه) ordered the man to inform his wife and give her the choice to stay or leave.

An infectious disease such as AIDS may cause infertility and it is also a means to transmit the disease to the child if not treated. Therefore, if this woman was given the option to leave her

---

[1] *Ṣaḥīḥ al-Bukhārī* 5707.

[2] Zād al-Ma'ād 5/165.

marriage because her husband could not bear children, this shows the wife has the option to leave the marriage if her husband has AIDS. This disease prevents the fulfillment of the purpose of marriage—including enjoyment, bearing children, love, and mercy—because it causes the healthy spouse to flee from the sick spouse similar to how one would flee from someone with leprosy. This disease also harms the person himself, and perhaps the offspring. Also, there is a known principle that states warding off a harm takes precedence over gaining a benefit.

There is also a principle in the *sharī'ah* that states "harm should be avoided," based on this principle a healthy wife will suffer great harm by remaining with a sick husband. And removing this harm is obligatory.

Another principle states, "Endure a specific harm to repel the general harm." Based upon this principle, it is clear that the harm the husband will endure by separating from his wife will be specific to him. But if the wife remains with him, the harm will increase and become a general harm that will affect the wife, the offspring, and spread among the community. Therefore, the husband should endure the specific harm that will only affect him in order to repel the general harm.

Another principle states, "When an affair becomes difficult, make allowances." The woman will experience severe hardship and restriction from every angle; and therefore, she is able to make allowances and request a separation from her husband. It is binding upon the husband to remove this difficulty and make things easy for her. Allāh (ﷻ) said:

﴿ فَإِنَّ مَعَ الْعُسْرِ يُسْرًا ﴿٥﴾ إِنَّ مَعَ الْعُسْرِ يُسْرًا ﴿٦﴾ ﴾

For indeed, with the hardship, there is relief, indeed with hardship there is relief.[1]

And He (ﷻ) said:

﴿ وَمَا جَعَلَ عَلَيْكُمْ فِي الدِّينِ مِنْ حَرَجٍ ﴿٧٨﴾ ﴾

He has not placed upon you in the religion any difficulty.[2]

What I see in this issue, based upon the reports of medical specialists about the seriousness of contagious disease—especially AIDS—and after the opinion of the jurists that if there is any danger, defect or disease that harms the wife, then she has the right to request annulment. These diseases are a valid reason for her to seek separation. The wife has the right to seek an annulment of the marriage and the husband should agree to it.

---

[1] Sūrah ash-Sharḥ 94:5-6.

[2] Sūrah al-Ḥajj 22:78.

Question: Is it permissible for the wife to request financial compensation from the husband afflicted with an infectious disease when she requests a marriage annulment?

This issue will fall under one of two scenarios.

Scenario One: The Disease Is Revealed Before the Marriage Is Consummated

If the disease is discovered, and the separation takes place before consummation, the compensation referred to will be the dowry. So does she have a share of it, since the husband is the cause of separation? In this scenario, the wife experiences emotional harm which is the divorce, and the extent of harm upon her dowry caused by separation due to his defect, discovered before consummation.

The scholars have two viewpoints on this.

First viewpoint: If the separation occurs due to a defect, before consummation or before they are alone with the opportunity to consummate, then the wife is due half of the agreed upon dowry. If the dowry was not mentioned, then she is given a fair compensation. A fair compensation is the maintenance given by the husband to his wife upon divorcing her. This is the viewpoint of the Hanafī scholars. The Malikī scholars agreed with this view if the husband says to his wife "I divorce you," based upon a defect he finds in her.

Second viewpoint: If the separation occurred before consummation, or before they are alone with the opportunity to consummate, the wife has no part of the dowry, whether the defect is in the husband or the wife. This is the viewpoint of the Shāfiʻī and Ḥanbalī scholars, and this was the opinion of Ibn Taymiyyah.

The first viewpoint is correct because the marital contract is complete if the pillars and conditions are fulfilled. And the healthy woman does not have the defect, but rather she affirmed the defect within the husband after the marriage. Therefore, he is the reason for the separation, even if she requests it. The consideration is given to the reality of the affair, not its outward appearance. Allāh (ﷻ) said:

﴿وَإِن طَلَّقْتُمُوهُنَّ مِن قَبْلِ أَن تَمَسُّوهُنَّ وَقَدْ فَرَضْتُمْ لَهُنَّ

فَرِيضَةً فَنِصْفُ مَا فَرَضْتُمْ ﴿٢٣٧﴾﴾

And if you divorce them before you have touched (had a sexual relation with) them, and you have appointed unto them the bridal, then pay half of that (bridal money).[1]

This noble verse refers to divorce before consummation, and this is the same situation as mentioned in the question. Likewise,

---

[1] Sūrah al-Baqarah 2:237.

Allāh (ﷻ) commands the husband to give his wife maintenance upon divorcing her. Allāh (ﷻ) said:

﴿ وَلِلْمُطَلَّقَاتِ مَتَاعٌ بِالْمَعْرُوفِ حَقًّا عَلَى الْمُتَّقِينَ ﴿٢٤١﴾ ﴾

> **And for divorced women, maintenance should be provided on reasonable scale. This is a duty on the pious.**[1]

From this verse we see that the husband should give his wife financial compensation if he divorces her, even before consummation. This proves the woman should also be given compensation if she discovers a defect within the husband before consummation because the woman was looking forward to marriage, she made preparations for it, and she was congratulated for her marriage. So, the sadness she will feel due to discovering the husband's defect is like the sadness she will feel due to divorce. Rather, her sadness will probably be greater because she will feel he deceived her, tricked her, and mislead her, if he was aware of his illness. Consequently, he compensates her feelings by giving her half of the dowry if it was mentioned, and a fair compensation if it was not mentioned. This fulfills the objective of the *sharī'ah.*

If the wife requests marital separation before the marriage was consummated due to the husband being afflicted with AIDS, the

---

[1] Sūrah al-Baqarah 2:241.

wife is due half of the dowry—if the dowry was mentioned as compensation—for the harm that befell her.

Scenario Two: The Disease Is Revealed After the Marriage Is Consummated

In this scenario, the disease was discovered and separation took place after the marriage was consummated or after they were alone together with the opportunity to consummate. In this scenario, the harm suffered from the wife is greater than in the first scenario because he consummated the marriage. He took her virginity, so she is no longer a virgin. The previously married woman is not like the virgin. In this case, does the wife deserve the dowry? And does she also deserve additional compensation?

The scholars, in general, have agreed that in the case of separation due to a defect, after consummation or after the spouses were alone together with the opportunity to consummate, the wife is due the dowry that was mentioned.

'Abū Ḥanifa and the Ḥanbalī scholars hold the view that if the separation is due to a defect within the husband, after the marriage has been consummated or after the spouses were alone having the opportunity to consummate, the wife receives the dowry in full if the dowry was mentioned. If it was not mentioned, she receives what women of her status normally receive.

'Abū Yūsūf[1] and Muḥammad ibn al-Ḥasan[2] said, "If the marriage was consummated, the woman is due the dowry in full if it was mentioned. If it was not mentioned, she is given what women of her status are normally given. If the marriage was not consummated, but they were alone and had the opportunity to consummate, the wife is given half of the dowry.

The Malikī scholars said, "If the wife requests the divorce due to a defect within her husband, even if she has a defect also, in this case she is due the dowry in full if her husband is someone who is able to have sexual intercourse. If he is not able to have sexual intercourse (such as a man who is castrated), there is no dowry due to her.

Shāfi'ī scholars said, "If the marital separation occurs after the marriage was consummated, while the defect was discovered between the marriage contract and the intercourse, and the wife was previously ignorant of it, then she receives a dowry like women of her status receive, while the mentioned dowry is dropped."

The correct opinion is that of 'Abū Ḥanifa and the Ḥanbalī scholars. If the separation is due to a defect within the husband, after the marriage has been consummated or after the spouses were alone

---

[1] Translator's note: Yaqūb ibn 'Ibrāhīm al-Anṣarī died 182 years after the migration.

[2] Translator's note: Muḥammad ibn al-Ḥasan as-Shaybānī died 189 years after the migration.

having the opportunity to consummate, the wife receives the dowry in full if the dowry was mentioned. If it was not mentioned, then she receives what women of her status normally receive.

Based upon that, if the separation occurs due to a defect within the husband such as AIDS, the wife is due the dowry in full if it was mentioned. If it was not mentioned at the time of the marriage contract, she is due what women of her status receive. This is because the divorce occurred after a valid marriage. And if not for the defect, the woman would have received the dowry at the time the marriage was consummated. Therefore, it is obligatory upon the husband to give her the dowry at the time of separation.

Question: Can the wife request additional compensation other than the dowry?

It is clear in this situation that the wife was harmed by contracting an infectious disease from her husband. This is from the greatest harms. This harm will be multiplied when the people—even her closest relatives—flee from her. Her reputation will suffer and she will have emotional damage as well. Even if it is decreed that she survives this disease, she will suffer in other ways. In most cases, she will remain unmarried as long as she has this infectious disease. And this is considered from the greatest harms.

There are two possible scenarios. The first case is if she contracted this disease. The second case is if she did not contract this disease, but she request compensation due to the damage to her reputation and emotional damage suffered due to this husband.

The consensus of scholars agree that a discretionary deterrent can be implemented against someone who harms others by statement or action. A discretionary deterrent is used when a crime is committed and there is no *sharī'ah* punishment for that crime, but the ruler wants to deter others from committing the same crime.

Ibn al-Qayyim viewed that the criminal's punishment should be the same as the crime he perpetrated against the victim, unless this punishment would involve something impermissible. This is closer to justice than to implement a discretionary punishment that is different than the crime perpetrated by the criminal.

In this situation, it is best for the ruler or judge to investigate the issue. Perhaps he may view it is best to give the criminal a similar punishment, or he may view it best to implement a different punishment.

Although the consensus of the scholars is that extra compensation should not be given, the ruler or judge may feel this is necessary due to the evil of the crime. Thus, they want to punish the husband twice by forcing him to return the dowry and give additional monetary compensation. They may also decide to force him to pay extra compensation to deter others in the community from committing the same offense.

Second Discussion: The Husband Who Does Not Have an Infectious Disease Requesting Compensation Upon Divorcing His Wife

We mentioned in the previous section that the wife has the right to request separation from her husband if it is discovered he has an infectious disease such as AIDS. In this section, we discuss the opposite. The husband is the one that is healthy and the wife is sick with an infectious disease. So, does the husband have the right to divorce her and request compensation from her due to this disease?

Scenario One: The Ruling on the Healthy Husband Divorcing His Sick Wife

The scholars have two viewpoints on this.

The first opinion states that each spouse has the right to request separation, be it the husband or the wife. This is the view of the majority of the scholars among the Malikīs, Shāfi'īs and Ḥanbalīs. This is also the view of Ibn Taymiyyah and his student Ibn al-Qayyim. This view has been narrated by 'Umar ibn al-Khaṭṭāb and his son, and Ibn 'Abbas, may Allāh (ﷻ) be pleased with them.

The second opinion states that it is not permissible to separate due to a defect, regardless of the defect. This was the viewpoint of the scholars who follow the Hanafī school of thought and those who understand the text upon its apparent meaning. Imām Shawkanī agreed with them in this opinion.

The correct opinion is that of the consensus of scholars, those who say it is permissible for the healthy husband to request separation from his sick wife. In some cases, this may be an obligation, because AIDS is not like other diseases. Rather, it is a catastrophe that remains with the person for their entire life and it can be spread from person to person.

Scenario Two: The Husband Requesting Compensation From His Wife

Some scholars hold the view the husband is entitled to seek separation, but he is not due compensation. Rather, his choice is either to remain with her or divorce her.

Other scholars believe the husband is entitled to compensation upon separation, but this has two scenarios based on if the marriage was consummated, or not.

The first scenario is if the husband requests compensation before the marriage is consummated and before he is alone with her, having the opportunity to consummate. There are two varying opinions for this scenario.

First opinion: The wife has no right to the dowry, and she must return the entire dowry to the husband because she is the cause of the separation. This is the opinion of the scholars from the Shāfiʿī and Ḥanbalī schools of thought.

Second opinion: The wife keeps half of the dowry if the husband separates from her by saying "I divorce you" before the marriage is consummated. This is the statement of the Malikī scholars.

The correct opinion is the first opinion, that the wife has no right to the dowry because the separation is due to a defect within her, and because the husband requests compensation before the marriage was consummated and before he was alone with her, having the opportunity to consummate.

The opinion of the Malikī scholars is strengthened if a healthy husband divorces his defective wife by pronouncing divorce without asking for compensation in the first place, nor asking a mediator to rule for him in separation. So, if he divorced her by himself without going through her guardian or a mediator, she is due half of the dowry. But if he divorces her through her guardian or a mediator, and they affirm that this is a significant defect, there is no dowry due to her, even if the separation was pronounced using the words "I divorce you."

The conclusion: If the healthy husband divorces his wife because she has an infectious disease before the marriage is consummated, and he requests compensation either through her guardian or the mediator, the wife should return the entire dowry and she has no right to any of it. The husband can also request that she return money he spent after the marital contract because she is the reason for the separation. But if he divorces her without requesting compensation, and this occurs before the marriage is consummated, the wife is due half of the dowry because the husband missed his opportunity to request compensation.

The second scenario is the husband requesting compensation from his wife due to a defect within her after consummation or after they were alone together having the opportunity to consummate.

The Hanafī scholars hold the view that if the husband divorces his wife due to a defect within her, after consummation or after they were alone together having the opportunity to consummate, the wife is due the dowry in full if the dowry was mentioned. If it was not mentioned, she is due what women of her status normally receive.

The Malikī scholars stated if the husband requests a divorce due to a defect within his wife, or if they both have a defect, the ruling will be based on the details of the situation.

If the guardian of the wife was aware of the defect within the woman under his care, and her affair was not hidden from him, such as her father, brother, or son, then it will be one of two scenarios.

First scenario: If the wife was present at the sitting of the marital contract, the husband has the choice to file his claim against the guardian or the wife because they participated in deceiving him. Thus, he can file a claim against either of them.

Second scenario: If the wife was not present during the sitting of the marital contract, the husband files his claim against her guardian, if her guardian is someone who knew of her affair such as her father, brother, or son, or even a non-relative if he was aware of her defect.

If the guardian of the wife was not aware of her defect and her affair was hidden from him because he was not her close relative, such as her cousin, a judge, or a proxy, it will be one of two scenarios.

First scenario: If the wife was not present during the sitting of the marriage contract, then the husband returns the affair to her guardian and requests something of payment from him. And the guardian is not to return to the wife requesting money to pay for his fine.

Second scenario: If the wife was present at the sitting of the marriage contract, the husband can only file his claim against her. The husband should allow her to keep a fourth of a dinar from her dowry so he will have paid something of the dowry.

Scholars from the Shāfiʿī school of thought state that if the separation is due to a defect found within the wife and it occurs after consummation, and the husband is ignorant of it, it will be one of two scenarios.

First scenario: If the defect is at the time of the marital contract, or if it occurs between the marital contract and consummation of the marriage, the wife is due a dowry similar to what women of her status would receive, while the dowry that was mentioned is waived. This is because the annulment of the marriage was based upon the defect that was present during the marital contract. Thus it became similar to an invalid marriage. Therefore, the husband does not return the dowry to the person that deceived him, whether it be the wife or her guardian.

Second scenario: If the defect occurred after the marital contract and consummation of the marriage, the wife is due the dowry that was mentioned in full because the dowry became obligatory with the marital contract and consummation, and it is not affected by what occurs after.

Scholars from the Ḥanbalī school of thought state that if the separation occurs due to a defect, and it is after the consummation of marriage or after kissing or touching with desire, then the wife is due the mentioned dowry. This is because the marriage was correct, meeting all its pillars and conditions, thus the ruling is based upon a valid marriage. The dowry is obligatory with the fulfillment of the contract, and it is established when the spouses are alone together. Therefore, it is not waived by what occurs afterwards.

The husband should file his claim against the person who deceived him, be it the wife or her guardian. 'Umar ibn al-Khaṭṭāb (ﷺ) said, "If a man marries a woman who is insane, or has leprosy or albinism, without being told of her condition by her guardian, and he copulates with her, she keeps her bride-money in its entirety. And her husband has damages against her guardian.

Mālik said, "The husband has damages against her guardian when the guardian is her father, brother, or one who is deemed to have knowledge of her condition. If the guardian who gives her in marriage is a nephew or a member of her tribe who is not deemed to have knowledge of her condition, there are no damages against him and the woman returns what she has taken of her dowry, and the husband leaves her whatever amount is thought to be fair.[1]

The correct viewpoint: The correct opinion is that of the scholars from the Malikī and Ḥanbalī schools of thought. They agree that the dowry should be return to the husband by the person that deceived him, whether it be the wife or the guardian who knew of the wife's defect. Based upon this, the healthy husband who learns that his wife has an infectious disease such as AIDS, after the marriage has been consummated or after they were alone with the opportunity to consummate—whether the disease appeared before consummation or after—he has the right to request the return of the dowry in full either from his wife or from those who deceived him.

---

[1] *Muwaṭṭā' Mālik* 1102.

Eighth Research: Child Custody

Custody in the Arabic language is from the word meaning incubation. A bird incubates its egg by putting it under its wings. The mother incubates her child by placing the child on her lap and raising and caring for the child. The parents are entrusted with the child, to raise him and take care of him.

The *sharī'ah* meaning of custody is to care for the person who is able to independently manage their affairs. Thus they are given an upbringing that is suitable for them.

The *sharī'ah* ruling of custody: Custody is obligatory because without it the child may perish or be harmed if not protected. It is an individual obligation upon a person if they are the only person that is capable of caring for the child or if the child will not accept anyone except them. It is a communal obligation if there are numerous people capable of caring for the child.

Rights of custody: Custody is for men and women who are entitled to it. But women take precedence over men because they are kind, compassionate, and more devoted to raising children. Then it goes to the men because they are more capable of protection, maintenance, and establishment of the interests of the young.

Child custody is shared by the parents if they are married. If they are divorced, custody goes to the mother according to the consensus of the scholars. This is based upon the *ḥadīth* of 'Abdullāh ibn 'Amr. He said:

أَنَّ اِمْرَأَةً قَالَتْ: يَا رَسُولَ اَللَّهِ! إِنَّ اِبْنِي هَذَا كَانَ بَطْنِي لَهُ وِعَاءً, وَثَدْيِي لَهُ سِقَاءً, وَحِجْرِي لَهُ حِوَاءً, وَإِنَّ أَبَاهُ طَلَّقَنِي, وَأَرَادَ أَنْ يَنْتَزِعَهُ مِنِّي. فَقَالَ لَهَا رَسُولُ اَللَّهِ – صلى الله عليه وسلم – "أَنْتِ أَحَقُّ بِهِ, مَا لَمْ تَنْكِحِي

A woman said, "O Messenger of Allāh, this son of mine, my womb was a receptacle for him, my breasts were a source of suckling for him, and my lap was a place for him to curl up in, yet his father has divorced me and wants to take him away from me." The Messenger of Allāh (ﷺ) replied to her, "You have more right to him as long as you do not remarry."[1]

Losing custody: Custody is revoked if there is something impeding custody or if the conditions or entitlement are removed, such as the mother marrying someone who is a stranger to the child,

---

[1] *Bulūgh al-Marām* 1151.

or if the guardian is suffering from a debilitating disease such as insanity, dementia, or a disease that harms the child such as leprosy. This is agreed upon by the majority of Hanafī, Shāfi'ī and Ḥanbalī jurists.

First Discussion: A Mother with an Infectious Disease Raising a Child Who Does Not Have a Disease

If the mother has an infectious disease such as AIDS, the specialists among the physicians stated two opinions on this issue.

The first opinion is by those who say that it is not medically proven that the infection is transmitted due to cohabitation and mingling between individuals. They stated, "Transmission of infectious disease among family members has not been proven, even if no additional precautions are taken except between the husband and wife. If the mother observes simple safety measures, she will not be a source of danger to her child.[1]

The second opinion is by those who say that precautions should be taken, and they mentioned that the intimate bond between mother and child differs from normal practices. And this intimate relationship may cause transmission of disease.

It is mentioned in the book *AIDS: the Plague of Our Generation*, "The infection occurs after birth as a result of the attachment and

---

[1] Dr. Muḥammad Haythm, *The Islamic Vision for the Communal Problem of AIDS.*

intimate connection between the child and its mother, or the affected father, often before symptoms appear."[1]

The scholars have differed on this issue based upon the differing of the medical specialists. Otherwise, the basis is custody or taking precautions based upon what is best for the child.

Statements of the early scholars:

According to the scholars from the Malikī school of thought, the male and female caretaker should be free of infectious disease. They said, "It is a condition for the caretaker to be of sound intellect, and they should not have leprosy or anything that is offensive to the smell or the sight or any type of defect that would frighten the child. The Prophet (ﷺ) said:

وَفِرَّ مِنْ الْمَجْذُومِ كَمَا تَفِرُّ مِنْ الأَسَدِ

One should run away from the leper as one runs away from a lion.[2]

Shāfi'ī and Ḥanbalī scholars have similar statements. They stated if the mother has leprosy and the child is not nursing, her custody rights should be waived."

[1] Dr. Muḥammad Bar, *AIDS: The Plague of Our Generation*," 79.
[2] *Ṣaḥīḥ al-Bukhārī* 5707.

Majd ad-Din ibn Taymiyyah[1] said, "If the mother has leprosy, she loses her custody rights." This is because it is feared the child will be affected through nursing from its infected mother.

Other scholars with similar views have stated that for every infectious disease that harms others such as leprosy, preventing them from mixing with healthy people, custody should be prevented. It is not permissible for people with leprosy to mix with healthy people in general, and the governors of affairs must prevent them from mixing with healthy people by providing a separate living accommodation for them. Based upon that, earlier scholars were of the view that the custody rights are waived if the mother has an infectious disease that could infect her child such as leprosy.

Statements of later-day scholars:

Modern day scholars have stated that if the child has no other guardian, the rights of the mother with an infectious disease should not be forfeited, although it is best that the child is distant from the infected person. The scholars differ if there are other available caretakers, but the closest relative is affected with an infectious disease. Based upon this, there are two opinions concerning this matter.

---

[1] Translator's note: Majd ad-Dīn is the grandfather of Shaykh al-Islām ibn Taymiyyah.

First Opinion: It Is Not Permissible to Forfeit the Custody of the Mother with an Infectious Disease

It was mentioned in the Islāmic Fiqh Council Decision Number 90 (7/9), regarding AIDS and the jurisprudential rulings related to the mother who has acquired immunodeficiency syndrome (AIDS), her custody, and breastfeeding of her healthy child: "Since the present medical information indicates that there is no clear risk presented from the mother with HIV infection caused from embracing and breastfeeding her healthy newborn, rather it is similar to regular contact and cohabitation, there is no legal objection to the mother embracing and breastfeeding her newborn unless there is a medical report preventing this."

It is clear from this that the council decided against removing custody unless there is a clear medical report stating the infectious disease is transmitted from mother to child.

Second Opinion: The Second Opinion Is That the Custody of a Mother Infected with AIDS Is Forfeited Until The Matter Is Clear

If it becomes clear that the infection is transmitted, she loses custody if there is someone who does not have an infectious disease to care for the child.

In the book *AIDS, Its ruling and the Connection Between the Family and the Community*, the statement to waive her custody until the matter becomes clear is valid. And I am inclined to say that until the matter becomes clear, it should take the ruling of leprosy. Until we are sure that it is not transmitted from person to person, the custody should go to someone healthy. But if there is no alternative, the child remains with the mother.

The correct opinion: The correct opinion is the child remains in the custody of its mother, because this fulfills the purpose of rearing the child with compassion and love. But this should be done using precaution, without intimate contact. And there should not be kissing in the mouth, to avoid transmission through saliva, although some doctors say it is not transmitted this way but it because it is possible this should be avoided.

Second Discussion: A Healthy Mother Raising a Child That Has an Infectious Disease

From what was previously mentioned, it is clear that the fear that a sick child could infect a healthy mother is the same as the fear that a sick mother could infect a healthy child. Except, the fear of a sick child infecting the mother is less and the premise is that the disease will not be transmitted. What was mentioned in the previous section applies here too, and even more so because the life of the mother has a greater importance than the life of the child because the mother is responsible for raising other children and fulfilling the rights of her husband. Therefore, the mother should take the same precautions as previously mentioned and avoid intimate contact and kissing the sick child in the mouth.

Third Discussion: A Father With a Disease Raising a Healthy Child

The father who is afflicted with an infectious disease may be the guardian of the healthy child. Perhaps the mother of the child is deceased or married to a new husband, or perhaps she is unable to raise her child for other reasons. The sick father has more right to raise his child in this situation. Based upon the aforementioned statements of medical specialists, jurists past and present, it is permissible for the father with an infectious disease to raise his healthy child. Based upon medical data there is no clear danger upon the child, but the father must take every precaution and practice safety measures and safeguard the child with the permission of Allāh (ﷻ).

Conclusion

All praises belong to Allāh, the One by Whom the good deeds are completed, and by His help the needs are fulfilled. May the salutations and peace be upon the leader of mankind and the Messenger of Islām, the one who left us upon a clear path, its day is like its night, no one turns away from it except that they are destroyed. And may the salutations be upon his companions and those that follow his Sunnah until the Day of Judgment.

In this research, I wanted to clarify some important matters that a Muslim woman needs in her marital and social life, and I thank Allāh for His success, help, and facilitation, and I ask Him more of His bounty.

My advice to Muslim women all over the world is to seek religious knowledge, as there is a great need to know it in order to defend Islām, especially on women's issues, and especially in our current time when the attacks on *sharīʿah* and its people, particularly women, have increased. The people today are far from Allāh (ﷻ). Allāh (ﷻ) has made clear the path that leads to Him, and that is by exerting effort and time to protect yourself from the traps of the devils from mankind and *jinn*. The Prophet (ﷺ) said:

مَنْ سَلَكَ طَرِيقًا يَلْتَمِسُ فِيهِ عِلْمًا سَهَّلَ اللَّهُ لَهُ طَرِيقًا إِلَى الْجَنَّةِ

Whoever takes a path upon which to obtain knowledge, Allāh makes the path to Paradise easy for him.[1]

That which I mentioned that was correct is from the success of the Most Generous. That which I said that was incorrect or due to forgetfulness was from me and the devil. And Allāh and His Messenger are free from it. I ask Allāh (ﷻ) to bless this research, and to benefit Muslim men and women in the East and West of the earth. I ask Allāh (ﷻ) to make it sincerely for His Face, and to accept it and to make it an argument for us and not against us. I ask Allāh to place it on the scale of good deeds, the day we meet Him. Our final supplication is all praises belong to Allāh, the Lord of all that exists, and may the salutation and peace be upon our Prophet Muḥammad and upon his family and companions collectively.

[1] Jami' at-Tirmidhī 2646.

Translator's Addendum

Question: From Rasheed Barbee to the noble Shaykh Shaykh Dr. 'Abdullāh al-Tayyār, As Salaamu alaikum wa rahmatuAllāh. May Allāh treat you well noble Shaykh.

Is it permissible for a healthy man, married to a healthy woman, to marry a second wife who has an infectious disease?

Answer: Wa alaikum Salaam wa rahmatuAllāh. All praises belong to Allāh, may the salutation and peace be upon the Messenger of Allāh. As to what follows:

Indeed, the *sharī'ah* states that a Muslim should not expose himself to calamity. Included in that is mixing with a sick person that has an infectious disease, especially if this disease is dangerous and chronic. The *sharī'ah* addresses both the sick and the healthy. 'Abū Huraira (ﷺ) narrated that the Messenger of Allāh (ﷺ) said:

لا يُورِدُ مُمْرِضٌ عَلَى مُصِحٍّ

The sick camels should not graze alongside the healthy ones.[1]

And 'Abū Huraira narrated that the Prophet (ﷺ) said:

وَفِرَّ مِنْ الْمَجْذُومِ كَمَا تَفِرُّ مِنْ الأَسَدِ

One should run away from the leper as one runs away from a lion.[2]

Leprosy is a well-known disease. We ask Allāh for safety and security. 'Amr ibn Sharid narrated that his father said, "When a delegation from the tribe of Thaqīf arrived to give their pledge of allegiance to the Prophet (ﷺ), there was a man with leprosy among them. He (ﷺ) said to them:

إِنَّا قَدْ بَايَعْنَاكَ فَارْجِعْ

We have accepted your allegiance, so you may go.[3]

His desire to marry this woman who is sick with an infectious disease may be due to the influence of emotion. He thinks he will be able to have patience and endure. Then when the calamity strikes, he will be remorseful at a time when remorse is of no benefit. There is no equivalent to safety. My advice to him is that he should not marry this woman. And Allāh knows best. May the

---

[1] *Ṣaḥīḥ Muslim* 2221.
[2] *Ṣaḥīḥ al-Bukhārī* 5707.
[3] *Ṣaḥīḥ Muslim* 2231.

salutation and peace be upon our Prophet Muḥammad and upon his family and companions collectively.